The Laughter of God

Other Writings by Walter Lanyon

Abd Allah, Teacher, Healer

And It Was Told of a Certain Potter

Behold the Man ◆ Demonstration

Embers ◆ The Eyes of the Blind

I Came ◆ The Impatient Dawn

Impressions of a Nomad

It Is Wonderful ◆ The Joy Bringer

A Lamp unto My Feet

Leaves of the Tree ◆ Life More Abundant

A Light Set upon a Hill

London Notes and Lectures

Out of the Clouds

A Royal Diadem

That Ye Might Have

The Temple Not Made with Hands

Thrust in the Sickle ◆ Treatment

Without the Smell of Fire

Your Heritage

Available through:
Mystics of the World
Eliot, Maine
www.mysticsoftheworld.com

The Laughter
of God

Walter C. Lanyon

The Laughter of God

Mystics of the World First Edition 2016
Published by Mystics of the World
ISBN-13: 978-0692643785 (Mystics of the World)
ISBN-10: 0692643788

For information contact:
Mystics of the World
Eliot, Maine
www.mysticsoftheworld.com

Photography by © Dr. Joel Murphy 2015
www.DrJMphotography.zenfolio.com
Printed by CreateSpace
Available from Mystics of the World and Amazon.com

৯০ ৵৶

Walter C. Lanyon, 1887 – 1967

Foreword

He will "fill thy mouth with laughing and thy lips with rejoicing."

And then one day I heard the Laughter of God in the midst of me and within the world, and all was suddenly changed. Old patterns and ideas were shattered and passed away—a new loveliness of life was exposed to view.

"God hath made me to laugh, so that all that hear will laugh with me."

Suddenly the leper broke into laughter—the filth of his mind slipped away. The sick, the lame and the halt suddenly laughed the Laughter of God and were healed—revealed.

And one day you will laugh the Laughter of God, too.

—Written in Germany
at Shining Lakes

Contents

Chapter One

The Laughter of God

God has made me to laugh, so that
all that hear will laugh with me.
—*Gen. 21:6*

Deep in my soul, I heard the Laughter of God, ringing in silvery cadences through the timbers of my being, breaking the human bonds and limitations as a strong yet gentle wind in the forest sweeps aside the strands of cobweb. The hard, fast knots that I had tied slipped loose, and the snarls of beliefs broke free. The river of my human life, frozen by a thousand and one false ideas and teachings, broke joyously into expression and went bounding to the infinite sea of Life, to be lost and found at the same time.

One dark cave of fear after another was illuminated by the light of this laughter, and swampy areas of sick thoughts were dried up instantly. Parched sands of hopelessness and futile efforts were drenched by the living waters, sucked in—absorbed instantly like a wave breaking on the sands. God laughing at me, and my puny efforts to make things happen—to make heaven appear, to attain the Sonship. Not the laugh of derision but of infinite compassion, a laughter so deep and sweet, so pure and glorious that everything in the nature of struggle gave way before it.

And the breath of that glorious laughter blew all the dirty rags of personal teaching and self-aggrandizement away from me. At first, the fierce joy that proceeded from the unheard-heard peals of laughter made me afraid — afraid that everything worthwhile was being taken from me and that I should be naked; but no sooner had the filthy rags of personality blown free than I was clothed in a panoply of light, and in this glorious raiment of light, I saw for the first time the glory of the Spirit made flesh.

I stood before the infinite peals of laughter, which flowed through all creation like floods of golden mist, filled with speechless wonder at the beauty of the world I had lived in—which had been invisible because of my separation, because of my personal ideas about attainment. I was as a child with a small measure at the seaside, trying to carry off a little water when the whole sea was at my disposal, and I understood for the first time the exhaustless sea of substance about me and that the idea of hoarding was but a childish fear grown into a Goliath by false teaching and beliefs. I suddenly became aware that the substance was everywhere, in everything, out of everything, and the only place of lack was in the hypnotic state of belief—and I alone created and moved in this vacuum.

And the glorious laughter rolled on, searching the very joints and marrow of me, dislodging every belief in fear, sickness, or age. As it swept over me and through me and round about me, I was amazed with the wonder of it—the fierce, terrible thing which was at the same time so beautiful and free. The wonder of it kept singing through my soul, as veil after veil of belief was rent asunder and new kingdoms stood revealed. The whole thing was as if one just saw a little deeper, as one looks through the surface reflection on a river and sees the pebbles and shells below, that was all. Only the Laughter made this possible, for it cleared away all the effort and straining which, in its attempt to see God, had been halted at the reflection on the surface instead of gazing into the limpid, glorious depth of Infinity.

The Voice, as Its honeyed tones flowed out like a burst of sunshine through storm clouds, was so unlabored, so untrammeled, and so divinely indifferent that It seemed to envelop me with an instant realization that all was well. No matter how many struggles had been made, no matter how many mistakes, how many shortcomings, how many failures, how long the belief, or how short the hate, it was all swept aside as nothing. The glorious, divine ease with which it was expressed made dis-ease impossible. It was the overturning—an overturning that had to take place before He, the Laughing One, could come into expression. The people of God are a people of joy, and it is not until they hear this God-laughter in their souls that they have attained to their heritage.

What of this race that speaks of the kingdom and doing the Father's work and uses all the language of the Truth, and at the same time sows seeds of fear and hellish inventions? What is this race that is always seeking evil to destroy, like a weasel seeks out a rat? What is the hopelessness they preach—that on one hand, you are the Sons of God, and that on the other, you must fight against evil of every sort and nature? "Ah, yes ... but ... if ... maybe ..." They roll these stumbling blocks under their tongues with a wise twinkle in their eyes, as much as to say, "Yes, it is all true, but it comes only with hard labor and long study, and it is not for such as you, sinner and worm of the dust that you are, until you have purified yourself in the fount of my wisdom and paid me personal homage."

And it is then that the Magdalene hears the Laughter of God and is clean and free—and in an instant too. It is when the cripple hears the Laughter of God that he leaps to his feet and runs away praising the living God. And it is when you—no matter where you are or what you are, no matter what you have done or left undone—hear the Laughter of the God within and the God without, that you will crash through the gates of hell and find heaven, no matter what these gates may be—person, place, or thing.

One moment's recognition that you are the Son of the living God, and you have attuned your ear for the Laughter of God, which will put to flight all the stupid ideas of *mine* and *thine* and free you into an expression that you have not yet dreamed of. How can you restrain the joy that fills you when you hear this laughter which, when it is heard, causes the winter of your discontent to break into full fruition; which causes you to see literally that "before they call I will answer" is not a bit of euphonious language but a positive, living, glowing fact.

"I was afraid," and therefore you were driven out of the garden of Life. You have been afraid that God will punish you; that it is too good to be true; that you are not ready; that it comes by great learning. And so you are still without the portals of your own kingdom, trying every way but the only way to re-enter. Many there be who try the way of violence, and many who expect to ride in on the skirts of another. There are some so foolish as to invite this.

Why do you not stop trying to get things, trying to learn how to get power, place? Why do you not come away from the man "whose breath is in his nostrils"—you who read this page—and go within and hear the Laughter of God and know that "it does not matter"—that the things which gave you great concern are all swept away into the dump heap? The sooner you learn this the sooner you will see they have no value. And one time, when you take away their value, they are possible of attainment to you. You profess to be a follower of the Master. If you in any way believe this, you will begin to listen for the Laughter of God through your whole being and will know that the Laughter of God sets you free from the snarling discontent of the tower of Babel in which you have been living.

Presently, as you listen for this Laughter, you will hear it, and gradually you will begin laughing — billows of laughter, silently-audible laughter that will shatter one limitation after another; laughter filled with the divine indifference that knows that the universe is filled with God and only God. To recognize this will cause this laughter to flow into expression and shatter the belief in sin, sickness, and death. And when this belief is shattered in you, the pictures of this on your universe are dissipated and are no more, and even the place thereof is no more. You will know why there can be naught but laughter in the kingdom of heaven. What good are words or arguments? What, in human sense, is a lecture worth on the subject of laughter as compared to one glorious, sudden peal of joy released by a God-soul and picked up by all those in hearing distance?

Gradually, as you learn of the Laughter of God and join in with the glory of the Sons of the living God, you will laugh at yourself. You will perhaps go back and laugh all the mistakes and faults and limitations out of existence. You will stand with your glorious feet on the mountaintops of Self-revelation, laughing at your universe and with your universe, laughing in words: "It is wonderful; it is wonderful; it is wonderful."

"Let the filthy be filthy still." Some may read into the Laughter of God a belief in carelessness and indifference, and some consecrated souls may rail and tear their hair and say that it is encouraging license and making nothing of sin in order that one may indulge in sin, and so on; for them this message is not.

He that hath ears shall hear what the Scripture saith unto the churches, and only he that hath a single eye is through with trying to twist meanings to suit personal ends. But he that hath the consciousness of the Son of the living God shall not find it strange that "he that is of too pure eyes to behold iniquity" should laugh at the belief in it that has bound men for so long; and this divine disregard does not in any way encourage license, but gives liberty to the Sons of God. It breaks up the dank morasses of human belief and reveals itself as heaven, a state of consciousness, which finds not happiness at the disposal of sin, health at the disposal of sickness, and harmony at the disposal of inharmony, but finds these pairs of opposites swept away. It finds man the individual Son of the living God, experiencing power and wisdom such as could not be put in human language.

The impress of the Divine upon the human causes the human to express in what, to the unenlightened thought, may seem to be a supernatural way. The how and why and when are all vested in the limited human concept of life.

When are you going to start laughing the Laughter of God? When are you going to join in the glorious chorus which is already encircling the globe and which has for its password, "It is wonderful"? You cannot stop this laughter once it is started; you will shatter the belief in disease in thousands as you go along your way — not by a poor, half-hearted way of beseeching God, but with the ringing Laughter of God in your Soul, which knows no sickness, sin, or disease and hence cannot look upon it. And in this very knowledge, it will impress the consciousness with the eternal well-being of the Son of the living God.

The man, if he hear the Laughter — that is, if he be willing to hear it instead of accepting the pinched human concepts of his human reasonings — shall break the bounds of his limitations; crash through the gates of brass; shake off the shackles of beliefs; burst through the prison bars of his own making, and find himself free, free, free, and find his soul ringing with laughter and with the song *"It is wonderful."*

Whoever you are who reads this page — you who sit in prison houses of disease, sin, and unhappiness — listen, listen, listen. *I* am the door of attainment. He will "fill thy mouth with laughing and thy lips with rejoicing." *I* am the door to this glorious Laughter of God. *I* am the way to the eternal bliss and harmony of the Sons of the living God. No matter where this finds you, nothing is hopeless or helpless; this joyous Laughter of the recognition of God, here and now, of the finished kingdom — of the sudden discovery that Jesus was not a liar but a truthsayer, a concrete truthsayer, when he said, "The kingdom of heaven is at hand; it is within you"—will cause this kingdom to descend out of the clouds of your belief and be real.

How can you help laughing silently and audibly the Laughter of God and see its ringing notes shatter the silly arguments about life? "The wisdom of man is foolish in the eyes of God." Why, try to measure the inspiration of the Almighty against any manmade teaching. "I will make you fishers of men." *I*, the I AM, when once discovered, will make the one who discovers it a fisher of men. Who can resist the Laughter of God—the fearless Laughter of God ringing through the universe, sweeping all the debris of human belief out of the way—no matter if it be thousands of years old and hoary with the respect of mankind?

Not one stone shall remain in place. The very foundations of the human belief shall be shaken in order that the true cornerstone, which has been rejected up to now, shall be laid. Yes, the stone, the very stone that the Master gave to us, the philosopher's stone, if you will—which we have rejected because to accept it would have been to overthrow great temples of human reasoning—will finally be made the head stone of the temple of Truth.

You are the temple of the living God, and from out the inner recesses of your being proceeds the Laughter of God. "The sons of God shout for joy." You will shout for joy, not because of victory over evil but because you have at last realized that the kingdom of heaven is not a place of overcoming evil but of revelation which is above the belief of a divided universe. "Awake, thou that sleepest, and Christ shall give thee light."

And I heard the Laughter of God in the Soul of my very being, ringing in glorious cadence throughout my universe, causing me suddenly to burst into a glorious laughter that was full of praise, full of wonder—full of wonder and amazement at that which I had missed through looking through a glass, darkly.

"Arise, shine, for thy light is come." Do you hear? *"It is wonderful! It is wonderful! It is wonderful!"* Heaven and earth are full of thee; sin, sickness, and death have vanished away. I *hear* the Laughter of God ringing in the deep recesses of your soul, you who read this page. I see the moving finger writing "It does not matter" across all the worries and fears of a lifetime, and I see this laughter writing the things of beauty over the walls of your temple and casting a glorious, glistening, white robe, a seamless robe of attainment, over you. And at last I hear you laughing from the mountain peak as you go on your way, without thought of scrip or purse or robe or ring or upper chamber; and long before you have reached your destination, the Laughter of God in your soul has gone ahead and made ready the upper chamber, and the Host has come out to receive you. Do you hear? You who read this page? You?

Under the aegis of Jesus Christ you can "go" with the Laughter of God in your heart.

Chapter Two

Rejoice, Thou Barren One

*For it is written, Rejoice, thou barren that bearest
not; break forth and cry, thou that travailest not:
for the desolate hath many more children than she
which hath an husband.*

—*Gal. 4:27*

Rejoice and be exceeding glad, "for the Lord
Omnipotent reigneth."

When we begin to see that the great universal
God overshadowing the universe causes it to bring
forth in due season, we begin to understand why it is
stated, as quoted above, that the barren and desolate
shall have many children. We begin to see that when
we contact the Father within, the old order of trying
to make things appear from the outside is done away
with. The old order passeth away—"Behold, I make
all things new," saith the Lord of Hosts.

Thousands of people have tried in every way to
bring forth the manifestation of Spirit—to make
demonstrations; yea, even to help others in the name
of the Lord—and have found themselves and their
lives barren as the *desert*, while others about them
seemed to bring forth many *children*. And they have
wondered, finally falling under the belief that the
manifestation of Spirit was not for them but only for

a special few; or that *they* were not fit avenues or not yet ready to express the Christ-Truth—hence, they bore no children.

But the old order changeth. The light is breaking over the dense human consciousness. Man is awakening to know that contact with the Father within is the propagating influence which will bring forth many more children than "she which hath an husband." He is beginning to understand that the creative force of the universe is even at this instant at work within the secret place of his being and that just as soon as he is ready to *let* (through the process of recognition), the Word will become flesh and dwell among them; he shall say, "Let the child be born," and the barrenness of a thousand lifetimes in the flesh shall be swallowed up in the glorious expression of the flowering desert. It shall "blossom as the rose." The well-watered garden shall take the place of the barren waste.

Martha had many cares in preparing to receive the physical Jesus. Symbolically speaking, the most she got for her work was perhaps a "thank you," while Mary feasted upon the hidden manna of Spirit. The human sense would like to condone poor, long-suffering Martha. A thousand reasons why she acted as she did are offered, but the rather uncompromising fact stands that she was rebuked and that the blessing was given to Mary. All this symbology does not mean that the Mary-consciousness might not do just as much work with her hands as the Martha, but from a different standpoint.

When we are on the outside of being, trying to bring forth, we are finally rebuked for our barrenness, even though we have put into expression the best that seemed to be in us. Likewise, the state that dreams of perfection and dwells in a mental state of rightness and perfection is also rebuked for vain imaginings. The Word must become flesh. "In my flesh shall I see God." One extreme is as bad as another. The Word must become flesh, and the flesh must become spiritualized, or resurrected, until the two become one. We then have Jesus the Christ—instead of Jesus the son of the carpenter and Christ the Son of God dwelling in one body. The two become one, and the sayings of the Scriptures are made true.

It is then that "death is swallowed up in victory" because death could only come to the one of a divided consciousness. What is told in secret shall be called from the housetop. Thus, we see that the Christ of God decided to submit to what is known as the Crucifixion in order that the world might see the transcending power of Spirit over matter and know that the law "I have power to pick it up and lay it down" was true and provable.

To stay on the heights of this law was to escape the seeming ugly reality. Do you imagine that the Christ, who was able to open the eyes of the blind, restore lost substance to the body of Lazarus, and do a thousand other things directly in opposition to the best accepted laws of the physical world of that day, could not have averted the Crucifixion? If so, then read Matthew 26:53:

> Thinkest thou that I cannot now pray to my Father, and he shall presently give me more than twelve legions of angels? (Matt. 26:53)

Where is the Father, and how do we pray? You see, then, that the Christ decreed this to come to pass. When He descended to the human Jesus state of consciousness, then He asked that the "cup pass from me." We understand that what He had accepted or decreed in secret should come to pass.

So is it true with you. You will begin to see that all the unborn children shall be released when the body and soul become one. To pray then will be to speak forth only that which is about to appear. Prayer will not be the old idea of wondering whether God wants to do a certain thing; it will be merely an exquisite feeling of gratitude, which says, "Thank you, Father," because it knows that the answer exists before the question.

Do you begin to see why it is that the one who was barren of manifestation will suddenly become fruitful? The limiting laws of the human concept of creation shall be dropped off, and the recognition of the Father of all shall cause thy barrenness to be a forgotten state. The former things shall pass away — they "shall not be remembered nor come into mind anymore." Thus, the barrenness shall be swallowed up in the abundance.

From the human standpoint, we even admit that we have teachers of Truth or music who cannot demonstrate for themselves but can give readily to others. From the divine elevation, this is an utter impossibility. This state of barrenness that brings forth no manifestation shall be fertilized with the overshadowing influence of the Ever-Presence, and what it has so long conceived on the invisible shall come into manifestation. No more shall the world be filled with barren ones who talk but who do not show forth the works, for they shall have united the body and soul and resurrected the risen Christ, which hath a body and which lives *in* the world but is not *of* the world insofar as coming under the hateful laws of the human mind. Death is swallowed up in victory, and with it all the things that go to bring about or make death possible.

"Call no man your father," for "every man is a liar, and the father of it." We see what lies have been told about us in the name of family, nationality, etc. We are burdened with hateful lies of every sort because we have recognized a human parenthood. We have assigned to ourselves all the limitations of humankind, and therefore, we are full of troubles, and so are our days. "Awake, thou that sleepest, and Christ shall give thee light."

Do you begin to see, oh barren one, that your name shall be changed and that you shall be as a land flowing with milk and honey? For the spirit of the Infinite Spirit broods over all and has broken the hateful bondage and set the prisoners free. Then is thy house gladsome with the laughter and joy of many children. Your glorious ideas that have so long remained in the silence of your mind come forth with joy and thanksgiving.

This is life eternal, to know Me. Where is this Me, and what will you do with this life eternal? Do you expect to carry on this limited personality for eternity? Do you expect to be John Smith for eternity? Only when Jesus the son of the carpenter became Jesus the Christ, the Son of God, did he ascend above the limiting influences of beliefs that belonged to his family, nationality, and time. When he became Jesus the Christ and "the Word became flesh," he transcended not only nationality but time and space and was able to set aside any law of the belief-world, just as the intense sunshine sets aside the dark shadows of night.

All disease and all barrenness out-pictured on your body and affairs are merely the shadows of beliefs cast upon the screen of your life. When the light has come, the shadows disappear. It is no good to throw a picture on a cinema screen if that screen is illuminated. So the shadows of the belief-world, which have been formerly true to the human mind, fail absolutely to record when you have come to the place of letting the light within "so shine before men."

We do not heal the Christ, nor yet prosper Him, nor yet change Him. We merely recognize Him, and as we do so, we bring out that which has been eternally.

Thus, healing is swallowed up in victory. Were anything real to be healed, it would be utterly impossible to accomplish it. The Christ of God needs no assistance, no help, no healing. But until the John Smith realizes this Christ within himself and permits It to come into manifestation, he will merely be working on a plane of imagination. Nothing concrete or definite can take place.

So many of us have stood about and seen the demonstrations; yea, we have even partaken of the bread, the fish, and the wine. But we have forgotten to partake of the Spirit, so when we had consumed the manifestation, we rushed back for more and found ourselves far from the source of substance.

So many people are so engrossed in listening to words that they only bask in the light of another's understanding and hence miss the glorious possibility of the command, "Go thou and do likewise." Many are asking for life free, which is promised, while still holding a miser's consciousness within themselves. Do you not know that until you can give yourself to the universe it cannot give the ever-flowing substance to you, for the simple reason that there is no capacity to receive it? The mind which is still hoarding cannot have the infinite rivers of abundance poured into it, else it would be destroyed; but the consciousness that has given itself to the Infinite is an open way through which the torrents and floods of substance can flow. It thereafter does not have to seek—it receives before it asks, for an infinite stream of substance is constantly pouring through into expression.

"It is written ..." So full of meaning is this statement that nothing shall retract or rub out a single word until it be fulfilled. "Not one jot or tittle shall be removed until the law shall be fulfilled." It is written that "the barren shall be more fruitful than she that hath an husband" — the law that is so full of promise and so glorious to all those who have wondered and grieved and tried to bring forth the works of the Master. "Go thou and do likewise" is a pretty big command, but there it is. What are you going to do about it? Talk it over with some wise one who will go into gushing phrases and words and whose barren life is filled with mute testimony of failure? Be still ... be very still. Finally you will hear the command, "Go within and shut the door," and you will let the glorious revelation take place within your own consciousness. "Nothing shall by any means hurt you." Who are you, and what are you going to do about it?

"And all nations shall call you blessed: for ye shall be a delightsome land, saith the Lord of Hosts" — ye, the newborn, the resurrected one. In the silence, in the tomb, in the aloneness, shall ye know the things which ordinarily are not written or spoken of — things which are neither seen nor heard by the noisy ones who are clamoring for place and power. "Behold, I make all things new." Do you see? You who read. All the nations shall call thee blessed, for they will recognize the Christ within you; the same glorious Christ that functioned in the man Jesus and enabled him to go against the laws of the human mind and set them aside as non-existent.

"None of them is lost but the son of perdition." The only thing that is lost is the memory of the human personality — the subconscious mind, the storehouse of all evil, the god that *was*. The god of the "kingdom of was" is lost, forgotten, wiped out, and the place thereof is no more. The holy presence of Christ in the eternal *now* is here. "Awake, thou that sleepest, and Christ shall give thee light." The desolate, barren land shall blossom as a rose.

> I counsel thee to buy of me gold tried in the fire, that thou mayest be rich (Rev. 3:18).

It seems a strange thing to say, "Buy gold in order that you may be rich." It would seem that if you had money with which to buy gold you would already be rich. But the secret doctrine causes the light to break over this symbology and to reveal that the complete giving up of the symbol is the buying of the gold that will make you rich. "Sell all that thou hast and give to the poor" is merely another way of stating that man is to take his attention away from the worship of symbols and place his allegiance on the Power. Awake, thou that sleepest.

> I counsel thee to buy of me gold tried in the fire, that thou mayest be rich; and white raiment, that thou mayest be clothed, and that the shame

29

of thy nakedness do not appear; and anoint thine eyes with eye-salve, that thou mayest see (Rev. 3:18).

Do you begin to see the treasures incorruptible that lie within the consciousness of Christ, awaiting the coming of the Master? Awaiting the coming of that one who will take his divine heritage and assume the proportions of the Son of the living God; the barren one who will suddenly realize that the Father—infinite, omnipotent, over-brooding all—has suddenly brought into manifestation the unborn children of desire. It is wonderful!

"Who is my father, mother, sister, or brother?" is the question you will answer with deep joy. Not to become a holier-than-thou but because you are ready to partake of the infinite nature of your divine Fathership. The wonder of the invisible shall be made manifest to you. You shall begin to partake of the qualities of Spirit. "As ye have borne the earthly image, so shall ye bear the heavenly." Do you hear? "Yet in my flesh shall I see God." It is wonderful!

"He that hath an ear, let him hear what the Spirit saith unto the churches." When you hear what It is saying to you (for you are the church of the living God, the center from which pours this glorious white light of revelation), then you will fold your tent and steal silently away into the new place of expression. And this shall be a natural event; not some human concept of moving out of evil conditions but a showing forth of the God-power into expression.

Do you see why "he that travels alone travels far"? And why the command "Salute no man" as thou passest along the highway is not unfriendliness but the essence of wisdom? "Behold, I make all (not some) things new." Do you believe that? Where is the *I*? What about it—you who read these lines? Are you going to run to someone and ask him to explain this to you, or are you going to be still and let *Me* explain and thereby turn your barrenness to fruitfulness and make you a gladsome land?

Just so soon as you begin to see the futility of opinions and beliefs regarding life and the Truth, just so soon will you go within and lave in the living waters and partake of the hidden manna and "buy gold that has been tried by fire."

"The old order passeth away" (Shakespeare). The old order is the order of your human personality and its destiny; the old law of cause and effect, of karma—the endless karma that you have been making and passing through. The Spirit of Life has suddenly thrown you off the wheel, and you are freed into expression as the Son of the living God. Do you suppose that the Son of the living God has anything to do with the son of the carpenter? He has only this much to do: to absorb the personal idea into the glorious, impersonal nature of God and thereby free him of the limitations and narrow confines, yea, the barrenness of the human concept of existence.

Hear ye, you who read this page: "But as many as received him, to them gave he power to become the sons of God." Do you hear? Do you see? When will you take your divine heritage? When will you appropriate the gifts of the Spirit? Not until you can go within and shut the door and listen not to the noisy man "whose breath is in his nostrils."

"And the Word was made flesh, and dwelt among us." So the unborn ideas that you have been holding in your mind, and wishing for all these many years, suddenly come into expression, for the Christ and Jesus are one. "Whatsoever things ye ask in my name, that give I unto thee." It is well.

> For it is written, Rejoice, thou barren that bearest not; break forth and cry, thou that travailest not; for the desolate hath many more children than she which hath an husband (Gal. 4:27).

Do you believe this? If so, you are at this very instant rejoicing. The rejoicing is a command and a statement of a fact at the same instant. You are automatically rejoicing because you have suddenly discovered that the barren years and efforts have been turned to good account and the glorious ideas have all been freed into expression.

When you come to the place of belief, you have come to the place of acceptance. You have come to the place where you have accepted the Reality of Being, and you are therefore not surprised, nor are you dismayed, at the appearance of the Power of Spirit which instantly neutralizes the beliefs of the flesh. "Let the dead bury their dead." So the old conditions and beliefs and acts all fall from the cliff of oblivion, and you stand on the heights, rejoicing in the name of the living God that is written on your forehead. You stand on the heights, not as one balanced for the space of a few joyous moments, to be dashed again into the valley of despond, but you stand there and rest in the new understanding that has shifted the weight of the human mind and beliefs and has freed itself from the law of human gravitation. "If ye be in the Spirit, ye are no more under the law." You are in the Spirit when you recognize the Christ within and act in accordance therewith.

The whole proposition is put to the one who seeks the light. When he has come to the place that he seeks not another's opinions and beliefs, then he has arrived at the point of:

> Verily, verily, I say unto you, he that heareth my word, and believeth on him that sent me, hath everlasting life, and shall not come into condemnation; but is passed from death unto life (John 5:24).

Here is a simple statement of a fact. "Believest thou this?" If so, you are beginning to experience a *new* life, a life that is everlasting, right here in the flesh, and *the* life which is now coming into manifestation cannot come under the condemnation of the former self. You are freed from the condemnation of the John Smith against which you fought so long. You are now passed from the death of these things— these beliefs and difficulties—into Life. Finally man is unveiled to himself. When agreement is made, conception takes place. The new idea or concept gathers quickly a body—and the child is born.

Chapter Three

Sound of Abundant Rain

Get thee up, eat and drink,
for there is a sound of abundance of rain.
—1 Kings 18:41

Thus spoke the prophet to Ahab. No one could believe such words; they were too good to be true. Three years had the scorching sun parched the ground, and the wells were dry and the riverbeds dusty highways. The brazen sky gave no evidence of it, and yet the prophet said, "There is a sound of abundant rain."

Ahab, running back and forth, looking for a sign and finding none, is representative of the person who is looking outside for signs and wonders. When the prophet makes a statement of a fact, it is in face of the direct opposite, as far as the testimony of the human sense is concerned. That is the reason for the insistence of "Be absent from the body," "Judge not from appearances," etc. There is a sound of abundant rain, the drenching downpour of Spirit onto the parched and dried life of any man. The more real the famine has been the more drenching the rain will appear, but what good is it to tell a person there is a sound of abundant rain when their cistern is dry and they are subsisting on a few cups of water? No good, because they can show you the reverse; not only can they show you the contrary but they can bring a thousand individuals who will verify every word they say. Further than this, they can even bring you men of learning who will prove by many arguments that it cannot possibly rain. And yet in the face of this, the prophet says, "There is a sound of abundant rain."

Finally, on the horizon of that brazen sky of despair, appeared a tiny cloud, as small as a man's hand. The prophet had spoken truly. "Faith is the substance (the very substance) of things hoped for, the evidence of things not seen." It is the evidence of the unseen, the unheard thing that is about to be released into expression. "Without faith it is impossible to please him." Unless you have faith in the principles of harmony, you will never become a musician, and you will never produce melody. Unless you have faith, which in the truest sense of the word is understanding, recognition, and acceptance of the unseen, you cannot bring into manifestation these things.

What is the good of saying, "There is a sound of abundant rain" if you only hope there is? What is the good of prayer that only hopes it will be answered? No more than applying the principles of mathematics in the same manner. "Before they call I will answer" is more than a pretty phrase. It is a statement of a fact to those who have ears and eyes; a statement that what they ask for already exists and is ready to come into manifestation in spite of the hateful appearances to the contrary—yea, though they be piled to the very heavens and be as adamant as the rock of Gibraltar. Asking, then, becomes a process of speaking the decreeing word. "Ye shall decree a thing, and it shall be established unto thee." Asking, then, takes on the nature of calling forth that which is.

"Let the dry land appear" is asking for something to appear which already exists in the unseen. But there is no doubt about its appearing; there is no looking for it to appear—there is the pure faith, or acceptance, that it is so.

We are only beginning to recognize what exists in the unseen and unheard world about us. The radio gives us ample proof of certain things that would have been emphatically denied by our forebears. That bacteria are being destroyed by the use of vibration would have utterly amazed our grandparents, as well as the fact that sound can be photographed, reproduced, and recognized as the voice of a certain individual. A piece of vulcanized rubber and a bit of steel can reproduce the voice of one long since passed from the mortal picture. Yet all these human devices are but playthings to the giant power of which we have heard so much through the man Jesus. We are only beginning to understand that "Judge not from appearances" is more than a religious adage.

"If ye have faith … ye shall say unto this mountain, Be thou removed and be thou cast into the sea." But if you have not faith, or recognition of the principle of God everywhere present, then your saying is but idle words that are clouds without rain. But if you have faith, "ye shall say" and "it shall be so." Do you hear? You who read this page? You?

Do you see why it is necessary to "go apart" to bide your own counsel? These things are not to be chattered about in the marketplace. They are reserved for the "upper room" of consciousness. If you desire them, the noisy voice must be silenced, and the asinine habit of setting the other fellow right, while you are full of obvious evils yourself, must stop. "I am the way" — walk thou in it.

When you recognize that the substance you are asking for already exists, then you too will be able to say to a barren earth, parched for many years with the scorching sun of failure and lack, "There is a sound of abundant rain" and believe it. What you discover in the invisible—what you recognize as true of God—will become true of the outer manifestation. "That which is told in secret shall be called from the housetops." Yea, "in my flesh shall I see God." But in order to see the manifestation of the rain, it must first be recognized in the invisible. "Eyes have not seen, ears have not heard, neither hath it entered into the heart of man the things that are prepared for them that love the Lord." The things that are prepared—when we recognize a thing from the spiritual standpoint of life, we will see it manifested in the visible world.

You are fed with the hidden manna that your fathers knew not of—your fathers, representing the old order of thinking, the old forms of metaphysics that are dead and that you are told to let alone. "Let the dead bury their dead." You have manna that they knew not of, for they had to see it with their eyes and handle it with their hands, and they received no blessing. Blessed are you because you have not needed a sign. You are blessed because you recognize that the Presence is everywhere, just as much in one place as another—everything in every place at the same time. "Awake, thou that sleepest, and Christ shall give thee light."

You are feeding upon the heavenly manna, and when you do this in silence, you will find that your material body is perfectly fed and cared for, and when you realize that you are clothed in the garments of praise and light, you will find the body clothed in perfect raiment. No wonder, then, you are invited not to consider the robes of the rich Solomon but the ways of a lily.

There is something most interesting in this. It is the manner in which the lily appears—out of the unseen; out of the invisible; out of the very substance which is about you now. No one thinks it strange when he plants a lily bulb that a lily should appear in due season. Why should it be strange, then, that prayer is actually answered?

The prayer is a thousand times surer of results than the lily bulb, when the prayer is one of recognition instead of one of begging and beseeching. Why should you think it strange that the much-needed rain should come to the desert? From the human standpoint, I know there are a thousand reasons why it should not come, and the testimony of the eye is anything but encouraging. It searches the dome of heaven and sees not a cloud, not a possibility of anything happening, and that is why you are told to "look not to appearances" as one of the first laws of bringing out the answer to true prayer.

When the acceptance is made in the invisible, there comes a joyous abandon. Not a careless abandon, or indifference, but a joyous abandon, for it has been decreed. The dark cloud as big as a man's hand that appears in the skies is enough to produce floods of rain, and so there is a joyous abandon. Hence, the command to the poor, tired, servant body, "Get thee up, eat and drink." In other words, rejoice and be happy, for everything is all right, and there is a sound of abundant rain. There is a glorious feeling of letting down, or resting and relaxing, when we have thrown the weight of our lives over onto the shoulders of the prophet—the Christ within.

Within the domain of everybody, there is that *something* that is symbolized by "the little cloud as large as a man's hand." You who read this page, you who have felt the hot, dry winds of futility and lost hope—in your life, that *something* is sufficient to produce it all and is within you now, awaiting recognition.

But the little cloud that is finally to produce the abundant rain has to be let alone, or else it will turn out to be a cloud without rain. Many a person has become anxious that God could not or would not do His work in the right manner and has turned back the abundant rain. Your anxiety for another, or for yourself, will only cause the famine to endure, for I have a way ye know not of. The I AM has a way that you cannot possibly feel or express. "My ways are not your ways. My ways are as high above your ways as the heaven is high above the earth."

"My ways are past finding out." Can you see, you who read this page? You?

"If ye have faith as a grain of mustard seed ..." You see, then, that the "little cloud" does exist in your life. Even the tiny little faith that caused you to venture to read this book is all that is necessary to flood your desert with the abundant rain of Spirit.

"Be not afraid; it is I." The I of Spirit is always with you, no matter where you go or what you do. It is at the hell of your own making, awaiting recognition, and It is at the uttermost parts or ends of the earth.

Note the word *abundant* in the first-mentioned idea. The expression of Spirit is always abundant; it is always full, pressed down and running over. It is lavish in the superabundance of Its expression. It is wonderful! The poor little measures that you have held to the universe are as nothing; they cannot hold the abundance of Spirit that is to be released by recognition.

Do you begin to see the abundance of Spirit? You are a spiritual being in a universe of Spirit. The flesh becomes spiritual by recognizing your true Self, and you are actually fed and sustained by the hidden manna. Just as soon as you know you are fed by the hidden manna, you will see the wholesome food manifested. For "what is told in secret is called from the housetops." Do you see? Do you hear? What, then, are you telling yourself? What you are telling yourself is what the world is retelling you, and many times that is what you are fighting.

You are fighting the echo of your own voice, your silent voice, which calls so loudly to the universe that people do not hear what you are saying with your lips. You argue with your own voice returned to you from the loudspeaker of the universe. You hear your own secrets broadcast in the universe. You fight against the injustice of your own secret findings. It is almost ghastly to contemplate, and yet it is glorious to know that it is so, for it immediately brings with it an opportunity of releasement.

What ye tell yourself in secret shall be called from the housetops. You are only telling yourself what you find to be true, and most of this you have found from judging from the appearance of things. Hence, when you begin to take your attention away from things and to be "absent from the body and present with the Lord," then will you begin to follow the commands of the Spirit, "Be still, and know that I am God." And when you are still, the still small

Voice is telling you things in secret that shall be proclaimed from the housetops—things that will make you thrill with joy; things that will bring out glorious new states of expression. So, little by little, we are finding that the way of attainment is not by struggling and torture, but by peace and contemplation of the realities and the recognition of the all-present God of love.

"There is a sound of abundant rain." This has come to you for a purpose. It has come to you to make you know the glorious revelation that is *even at this moment* being made manifest to you, the abundant rain of substance into your life. If the desert be one of sickness and lack of strength, then the abundant rains bring, even at this instant, the flood of health, vitality, and power. If the desert be one of loneliness and futility, then the abundant rains bring floods of joy, thanksgiving, and attainment. Heavenly new fields of expression open before you. The veil drops from your eyes, and you see the reason for many things; the blinding sense of futility has passed away. If it be the desert of financial lack or limitation, then the flooding rains will be in terms of substance suitable to meet all the needs. "Ye shall know the truth, and the truth shall make you free." It will make you free from the beliefs of the human sense, free from your own limitations, different for each man in accordance with his present need.

It is glorious, thrilling. Listen … listen … listen … you who read this page. Listen … listen … listen.

"There is a sound of abundant rain." There is a sound of abundant rain — the downpour of spiritual substance in any form that is necessary to neutralize the desert of your belief. Glorious, glorious truth. It is well with thee. You are in the floods of Light and Life. On the invisible, you are feeding on the manna that is hidden; at this very instant, you are clothed in the garments of light and thanksgiving. It is wonderful. It is glorious. You are in the flood of Spirit, of Light, of attainment. "Heaven and earth are full of thee" from glory to glory. You go on into more wonderful fields of realization.

One moment of recognition, one grain of faith as big as a mustard seed, and you have brought in the harvest of substance. If it be to that place filled with inharmony, you will see the floods of harmony and understanding descending. If it be to the place of pain, then the healthful power of life shall quicken the body. It is wonderful.

Listen ... listen ... listen. There is a sound of abundant rain. Even as I write and you read, there is a sound of abundant rain in the form that you can best appreciate and understand it. There is a sound of abundant rain, and the desert that is loaded with seed is to blossom as a rose, is to run a riot of glorious colors and perfumes, where once the wind tumbled the dry sagebrush over burning sands. Yes, it is all there. "The mouth of the Lord hath spoken it." The sound of abundant rain is at this instant audible to

your inner ear. Fear not. Be not anxious. It is well—
the downpour of Spirit is at this instant upon you.

You listen, *this time* to the silent Voice within.
You begin to hear, to act, to "go," having heard "I go
before you." It is wonderful when you *listen*.

Chapter Four

Silver and Gold

Silver and gold have I none; but such as I have
give I thee ... rise up and walk.

A beggar sitting 40 years at the Temple Beautiful asking for silver and gold. What for? To consume, and then ask for more. The endless getting and using and being obliged to get more; the endless making of demonstrations; the endless asking for the loaf of bread that is consumed immediately — the endless looking for symbols instead of getting back of them. Why didn't he go into the Temple Beautiful?

Picture the cripple at the temple gate. For years he has been there. He has long since accepted his infirmity as his natural heritage, so he begs for a bit of silver. Picture the disciples, knowing that if they threw him a handful of gold or silver, they were only doing what hundreds of others had done in a more or less degree; that in reality, they would not help him. At best, it would only be a temporary relief.

"Silver and gold have I none; but such as I have give I thee," and then followed the gift of healing.

How much silver and gold would it have taken to bring that healing in the marts of the world? More than likely, from worldly standards, it was beyond price. More than likely, the body of that cripple was in such an emaciated state that if the healing were possible, it would have taken years to bring the cripple back to normal—back to normal by the knife, by food diet, exercise, and long, long months of convalescing.

"Silver and gold I have none; but such as I have give I thee—Arise! "

The bestowal of the gift instantly rehabilitated the disease-laden body. Instantly the cripple accepted the priceless gift, leaped up and ran, rejoicing and singing. Picture the same cripple with a handful of gold. His joy might be increased for a moment, but he would soon return to his former limitation.

Note that the gift was instantly accepted. And what was the gift? It was the full recognition of the presence of the Power of God in the midst of him. Every man has the gift. He learns that the gift is beyond the price of fine gold or rubies. Silver and gold and fine rubies become as worthless chattels in face of the priceless gift that every man has to give to the world—yea, to give to himself. Arise!

Yet the world is full of cripples who sit at the gates of their own temple and beg for silver and gold. The world passes by and throws them a copper or two; but sooner or later one comes by and says, "Silver and gold have I none; but such as I have give I thee," and it is at that moment that the beggar has within his grasp complete freedom from the beggardom he has so long accepted. Arise!

Unless, however, he accepts his gift, he will remain at the gates of his own temple, begging the crowd of human thoughts that go by for enough to live on. Always seeking the symbol instead of what is back of it, always looking for the loaves and fishes, makes the eyes more blind and the ears more deaf.

Looking to outside conditions for help will result in defeat. After you have consumed the loaf of bread, you are hungry again and must get another, and thus goes the game of life—devoid of charm, as crude and misshapen as a statue hacked from a block of wood with a clumsy garden axe.

Hypnotized to the human thinking, man has accepted his state as one which cannot be helped. He blames his heredity, prenatal influence, environment, accident, or disease. But all or any of these might have entered into the case of the aforementioned cripple, and still they did not act as a wall against the showing forth of the priceless gift of Spirit. No law that man has made is a law to Spirit, and as soon as man looks away from the symbols, he will receive the gift of Spirit and will understand why the priceless gift is not in dollars and cents but in the substance which lies behind them.

> When the Son of man cometh, shall he find faith on the earth? (Luke 18:8).

When the inspiration of the Almighty speaks to you and gives you the priceless gift, can you take it? Can you take your good in the same degree that the cripple at the temple gate accepted that which was given him? It was a tremendous gift that he took, from the standpoint of his bodily condition. It meant that a great physical change had to be made instantly. It meant that the well-nigh impossible had to happen.

It meant that he had to let go of a lifetime of hypnotism of human thought. It meant that it was opposed to every single human law and was placed in the category of the impossible. It meant that it was sweeping aside, like so many cobwebs, laws that were hoary with age and concreted with millions of proofs.

Yes, it meant all these. And it means that the condition that you may be under can be no more difficult than this single instance that is given you. It also means that the change which is necessary to bring you from the darkness into the light will be no greater, no more difficult or impossible of attainment, than that performed on the cripple at the temple gate. Arise!

Even at this instant, "Behold, I stand at the door and knock." The very *I* that spoke through the disciples and said, "Silver and gold have I none," the very revelation of your perfect health and freedom, stands offering you the gift of life and happiness, offering you freedom from the human bondage, no matter how long it has been with you. "Is there any thing too hard for me?" Is there anything that is difficult for the power of the All-God within you to bring forth into manifestation? Arise!

What is this seeming opposition that seems so much more powerful than God? Awake, awake, awake! Arise and shine! The thought that has been trailing its wings in the mud of human existence will scale the heights of interstellar space.

You will note in the case of the beggar, and in the case of many others instantaneously healed by the Master and his disciples, that the healing took place almost before they had time to think. A gift is accepted at the instant it is presented. When we stop for a moment to reason, "Could this happen to me?" we are lost. God has power sufficient to instantly offset the oldest and most terrible human concept of law. "Fear not; it is I." Arise!

"Silver and gold have I none" does not in any sense of the word imply poverty or lack on the part of the disciples. They might have added, "Silver and gold have I none—*for thee*," knowing that it would not in any way help. When they ask for bread, *I* will not give a stone. The glorious help which enables a man to see his true Self is more precious than a handful of gold or a world of human sympathy. Arise!

Most people are beggars in life. Not all of them sit at the temple gates asking for gold, but they are begging for other gifts, or the symbols of other gifts, and missing the glorious gifts of Spirit that are poured out upon them. So hypnotized to the outside manifestation are they that they fail to see or hear the gift that is bestowed upon them. Symbols, always symbols, until they learn that a symbol without something back of it to animate it is nothing but a puppet; it has no power nor life nor expression.

Beggar of life, when will you begin to accept the gifts of the Father? When will you accept your divine heritage and rise from the degrading position and let the light of revelation pour over you in flooding streams? Arise!

When will you come out of the old Pauline doctrine of "Work out your own salvation with fear and trembling" and accept the glorious gift of God, "Fear not … it is your Father's good pleasure to give you the kingdom of heaven"? A gift—yea, even a gift as large as the kingdom of heaven—must be accepted.

Think of it, beloved—the trembling and fear, the working out of your own salvation, is suddenly all set aside by the acceptance of the gift of God—the kingdom of heaven. And just as the cripple at the temple gates ran and leaped for joy into his new state of expression, leaped out of years of belief of sickness, ugliness, and filth, leaped into freedom and left behind him all the things that were true of the crippled beggar, so you, Son of the living God, will make the transformation from the present state of sickness, poverty, and unhappiness into the perfect heaven of harmony and bliss. When will you accept your gift? When will *you* arise?

It is your Father's good pleasure to give you the kingdom. Where is your Father? What did Jesus the Master say of this? "The Father within me, he doeth the works." The Father-Consciousness within you is that which will give you, the human body manifestation, the kingdom of heaven here and now. Do you see that it is not something afar off that is going to grant this favor to you? "Yet in my flesh shall I see God"; yet in the present body shall you see the glorious revelation because soul and body have become one, and "whom the Lord hath joined together, let no man put asunder."

> Stir up the gift of God which is within thee" (2 Tim. 1:6). Arise.

In the midst of your chaotic world is the gift of God—the gift of Life eternal, the gift of the infinite riches of the kingdom, the gift of increasing the manifestation. Stir up the gift of God which is within thee. It is already there—the gift of beautiful life, glorious life, radiant life.

And in turn, the beggar goes his way rejoicing and giving in turn the gift. We are afraid of the gift; we make a sickly attempt at speaking the word. We wonder if God would want us to assume such authority and such proportions, and at the same time we acknowledge, "I am the Son of the living God."

> When the Son of man cometh, shall he find faith on the earth? (Luke 18:8).

This is addressed directly to you—you who read this page: if the prayer that you asked this morning suddenly came bounding out into expression, would you be ready and willing to accept it? If the piece of gold that you had asked for could actually come into manifestation, would you be able to accept it, or would you have to look to see whether it had a serial number, or whether it were in accord with the human intellect? If you were suddenly to have the gift you were asking for made manifest, could you have faith enough to accept it? Until the perfect acceptance can come and the curiosity has been absorbed in the absolute faith that "all things are possible to God," these things cannot be, no matter what a thousand voices may say pro or con on the subject. Arise!

If you should tear the hide from a living body to see how the life was produced underneath, you have no life. The killing of the goose that laid the golden egg is the result of curiosity. If you are secretly cherishing in your mind such ideas, you will see nothing, for nothing shall be there. The soul is not curious—it knows. *I* have a way that you know not of. The I AM has Its way that no human intellect can see, understand, or believe. Arise!

The whole glorious proposition lies within yourself. It is asked of you, "When the Son of man cometh, shall he find faith on the earth (your consciousness)?" You have to answer that for yourself. It does not make any difference what the answer be so far as the outside world is concerned. It is, however, tremendously important to you. What would you think? If the prayer you have just asked were at this instant to be fulfilled, could you—you who read this—accept it?

Be still, and know that *I* am God.

Chapter Five

No Enchantment

Surely there is no enchantment against Jacob, neither is there any divination against Israel.

—Num. 23:23

"I will overturn and overturn ... until he come whose right it is" (Ezek. 21:27).

This is the day when much is said about enchantment and divination—sometimes openly under these names, but more often referred to only or spoken of by a new modern name. The mad enchantment of a bird and a serpent is only equaled by the enchantment that exists between man and the serpent of human thinking. The only way for the bird to break the spell is to take its eyes away from the fearsome thing upon which it is gazing. Likewise, the only way for man to break the spell of disease, hate, fear, sin, and lack is to take his attention away from appearances, being "absent from the body and present with the Lord" and judging "not according to the appearance," but judging "righteous judgment" —the scriptural means of breaking the enchantment. But few people want to follow these commands. They want their problem clearly stated and set forth, and then they want the remedy. They want to attack the evil and destroy it, and so they are destroyed by the very thing they desire to destroy.

"But," says one, "that is the very reason I took up the study of Truth—I want to destroy the evil in my life." There is nothing in My kingdom that can or shall be destroyed, and the appearance you are attempting to destroy is the out-picturing of your own belief. You are attempting to destroy it while you are constantly creating it by gazing at and handling it and examining the nature of it. Many people who are seeking God are turned awry over the appearances of a few leaves in a teacup or a few lines on the hand or other outside things. They will ask anyone to forecast the future and are much more willing to believe those prognostications than to accept the fact that "God's in His heaven (state of consciousness), all's right with the world" (Browning).

In spite of the statement "No man knoweth what a day brings forth," in spite of all the eloquent declarations that God is the only power, just let the idea of "fortune" be mentioned, and they are all ears—being much more willing to take the word of a person who is prostituting the sacred gifts of Life than to have the revelation of their inner soul made manifest to them. "Broad is the way that leadeth to destruction." The flower-strewn way of hearing good things that are about to happen by chance leads them on; they wade knee-deep in glorious flower-covered fields, snatching a posy here and there, thinking how wonderful it is that their "fortune" is so fine, perfectly unaware of the poisonous serpent that suddenly makes itself manifest in the form of a horrid prediction. Then they want to escape it all and fly back into the idea of Truth and loudly proclaim that "God is All." But the enchantment has done its work.

The flowers of the spurious joy of delving into the future have withered in their hands or turned to thistles. They shriek, "Save me." The terror of seeking those things which are an abomination to the Lord is their portion, yet even in this time of terror, even in this time of desolation, there is always the way of escape.

Why is it that people who profess God as the only power wish to hear of other forces which they seem to think are actually more powerful than God? What is the insane curiosity of looking ahead, trying to see if something good is going to happen, but the hypnotism of the human mind and the failure to awaken to the glorious *now* of life? Anyone who has awakened to the Christ-Consciousness is not looking for the good that is to come; he is reveling in the glorious present of the *now*, and he does not doubt the future. He is not wondering if things will be taken care of. He knows that as long as he stays at the point of the *now* of God, he will not need to prepare to destroy the devil.

If you are looking for good to come in the future, you are still where you were before you heard the Truth. Do not the Gentiles do that? What difference if you have let go of the old idea of heaven, with angels, if you still hold on to the false idea of evil being more powerful than God? What is this belief of a power opposed to God? Why is it that because someone has prophesied truly for ten thousand people who were under the enchantment of human doctrine, you, the Son of the living God, newly awakened to the powers and the gifts of the Spirit, should come under the sway of this lie?

Did not the magicians, soothsayers, and wise men produce a serpent after the prophet had produced it as a sign, and did not the appearances show clearly that the power used by the magicians was the same as that used by the man of God? Yea, it was terrific proof, enough to make the stoutest heart faint for fear of the power of evil. But did not the serpent of the man of God suddenly devour all the serpents of the magicians, and is there not hidden in this glorious proof that God is supreme to the belief of any man or any teaching or any idea, however hoary with age and respect they may be? "There is no enchantment against Jacob, neither is there any divination against Israel."

"Awake, thou that sleepest, and Christ shall give thee light." Awake from the hypnotism of human belief and break the spell it has cast over you. Realize once, for all time, that "He who watches over Israel neither slumbers nor sleeps," that the I AM Consciousness watching over you neither slumbers nor sleeps and you are eternally in His care. You are the Son of the living God, and this glorious recognition causes the laws of the human belief, however powerful they may have seemed, to give way before the new dawn. Awake, awake, awake. It is well with you!

Are you true to your own word? Then the whole world (your universe) will be true to its word. *My* words are Spirit and they are Truth, and "they shall not (positively not) return unto me void, but shall accomplish whereunto they are sent."

You may be under the enchantment of money. "A rich man shall hardly enter the kingdom of heaven." Not that money is bad; it is the love of money that is spoken of as the root of all (not some) evil. It is the enchantment again of looking upon the outside and imagining that there is power there. There is no buying power in the symbol of money; it is what is back of it, for, even while you hold the symbol in your hand, it may decrease in value to a point where it is not worth the paper it is printed upon. The enchantment of money is due to the fact that we have placed power in the symbol instead of placing it where it belongs. Hence, the saying "Money is power."

But what of a dying man who has exhausted the finest arts and crafts that money can buy? What about friendship? What about love? What about anything that really matters in life? Looking on the symbol, people become enchanted by it, then think to possess it but end by being possessed by it; they are destroyed by the serpent just as surely as the bird is.

Trying to demonstrate symbols of money has not proven successful. Perhaps in a few remote cases it has been done; a handful of gold has been forthcoming—and then the terrible lapse that has followed and the wonder how it happened and why it does not happen again. Keeping your attention fixed on things will keep them from you. As you pursue them, they flee before you as the mirage in the desert that seems so real and true.

Power is not in the symbol; the substance of money is not in the dollar bill. The golden idol with feet of clay will crash upon your own head. The worship of the golden calf seems to be in accord with the masses of humanity, but it brings the sharp rebuke, "Thou shalt have no (not any) other gods before me." Where is this Me and what is the Me that comes before all else, except the I AM Consciousness within you, which is your point of contact with the universal Whole?

"To him that hath shall be given" does not seem fair, and is not fair from the human standard of things, but it is true. To him that hath the consciousness shall be added symbols of that consciousness, not because he needs them or because he is receiving a special favor but because he is automatically functioning a law of God. "With all thy getting, get understanding." But most people say, "With all thy getting, get gold, then you will be able to go into the world and take possession."

There is no enchantment against Jacob. There is no law of poverty that is fixed over you, through which you are obliged to function. No, not if ten thousand wise men say as much. You are the Son of the living God—the All-Power—and when you recognize this, then will you understand how there can be no enchantment against Jacob.

"If ye seek me after the loaves and fishes, ye shall not find me" is recorded as the saying of the Master. If you are seeking the things, then you will come under the enchantment of things, and you will reap the result of this divided allegiance.

"Who by taking thought can add one cubit to his stature?" You may answer the question yourself—and look over that which follows; perhaps through the crannies you will see the light and hear the command, "consider the lilies and the ravens and the sparrows" and many more things, and see that you, as the Son of the living God, are not dependent upon the divination of the human mind.

Neither shall you be under the enchantment of disease, for the Son of the living God is a being of pure Spirit and is made of the substance which comes under the direct control of God, who is of "too pure eyes to behold iniquity." Pause a moment and ask yourself whether there possibly could be an actual law of sickness and misery, and if so, why have you, of all people, been singled out to manifest it? You can only answer that it is because of your acceptance of this law as a power beside which God Himself is powerless.

The more you look at the loathsome manifestation the more real it becomes and the more you realize the utter impossibility of escaping it. Who can gaze at disease in its various forms and even imagine how it could be relieved? Yet in turning away from the appearance lies a sudden and sure escape—just as you know that the bird with two strong wings has an instantaneous means of escape from the serpent; yet so long as it stands gazing at the object of its fear, just so long will it be in the grip of that thing.

Take your attention away from the appearance and place it on the All-God, and you will find wings to escape any difficulty to which your human thinking has brought you. Awake, thou that sleepest—Christ is risen. The Christ-Consciousness within you has risen out of the tomb of your own making, and He comes with all power. Turn your attention away from appearances, and the enchantment will be broken.

> Surely there is no enchantment against Jacob,
> neither is there any divination against Israel.

Either God is all-powerful and able to do all things, or else our teaching is in vain.

"There is therefore now no condemnation to them which are in Christ Jesus." When we begin to read the words of light and see the inner meaning, we see that the enchantment of the human mind is broken and that the condemnation of the evil of our beliefs is cancelled, and we are freed into the Spirit of the sons of the living God. When we forsake the evil in our consciousness, then it is forgiven and released; the condemnation goes with it, and we are freed. Awake, thou that sleepest, and Christ shall give thee light.

Are you looking for a lucky charm, a sign, or a miracle? Miracles happen only to the human belief. The operation of the divine Mind, producing health where the human mind sees sickness, and prosperity where the human mind sees poverty, is a natural process. It is only unnatural to the relative world. The statement "Signs shall follow, they shall not precede" does not mean anything to the person who is always looking for things. He wonders why, after years and years of serving God, he has never experienced a miracle or a revelation. Awake, thou that sleepest; the signs follow, they do not precede. Do not seek Me after the loaves and fishes because as soon as the loaves and fishes are consumed you will be without them and be the creature of chance again. There can be no chance in the law of God, else the very harmony of the universe would be destroyed. There is no power opposed to God.

In Nigeria, all sorts of black magic is practiced, with the most terrible results. But in every instance, the person who is to receive the baneful effects of this so-called power must be informed that it is being used against him, and this alone tells the tale.

Not that which goeth into a man defileth him, but that which cometh out. It is not what you take in that counts but that which comes out. If you hear evil and accept it, it comes out in the form of evil in your universe; therefore, it is that which defileth you. If disease is real, then it must come into manifestation.

Surely there is no enchantment against Jacob, neither is there any divination against Israel.

The only enchantment in any of the evil lies in the fact that your attention is fixed upon it, and so it becomes real to you; but as soon as you take your attention away from it and place your consciousness on God, the enchantment is broken.

We look out upon a universe of our own making. "To the pure all things are pure." "Let the filthy be filthy still." "What thou beest, that thou seest." The one who is perpetually looking for the clay feet of others stands on crumpling feet and falls in his own dust. "Be ye wise as serpents and harmless as doves." "Occupy till I come." "I come quickly."

It is well. A newer courage suddenly comes into being, a fearless *believing*, a divine indifference.

Chapter Six

Then Went He In and Shut the Door

"Then went he in, and shut the door" (2 Kings 4:33). What goes on behind the closed doors is going to be of tremendous interest to the outside world. "That which is told in secret is called from the housetops." When you think of the word *secret*, you think of the closed door—you think of the "secret place of the most High." In fact, you think of the center of Being. Until a man learns the law of silence, he cannot leave his burning desert of human experience.

He that travels alone shall travel far; he that holdeth his tongue shall take a city (a new state of consciousness), and so he who learns to "come out from among them and be separate" is getting his feet firmly placed on the ladder that leads safely to heaven—realization.

Power is noiseless; its manifestation may make a terrific tumult, but power of itself is noiseless. "Be still, and know that I am God" has been a command which has been as little heeded as the one "Before they ask I will answer"—but that also bespeaks silence accomplishing something that noise could not. The burning coal which is placed on the lips seals them forever, and it is to such a one that power is given— given because he has discovered something in the silence that he can never discover anywhere else. He has found certain secret springs which, when released, will cause the whole face of his universe to change, and people will say, "It is a miracle," but he will know differently.

Until man learns the law of silence, he will travel on in the heat of the burning desert of experience, comparing notes with others; discussing and arguing about the vital truths which never seem to work and yet seem so plausible and real.

"I do not see why it is that I cannot make more progress. I have been faithful; I have helped many; I have heard hundreds of lectures; I have read hundreds of books; I have given of my substance—and am still in this terrible condition."

The answer to all this is simple, yet it will be rejected by many because they like to "talk it over" first with someone who is supposed to know more than they do; then they want to talk it over with God and tell Him just what to do before things will be right in the universe. But nothing happens, and they either go down into the ditch of human failure or hear the "still small voice," which constantly says, "Be still … be still … be still, and know that I am God."

"In quietness and confidence shall be thy strength." A thousand times that is read over, and by the very one who is seeking light and under-standing—but will you obey it? Nay! nay! You will pass it over and go again into the desert of human hope, seeking for shade and water. In the desert through which you are traveling is the deep, secret well of silence, and when you drink the waters thereof, you are refreshed, and the water therefrom will transform the desert into a garden.

"Be still" —be very still, and *know* that *I* am God, and you will find out something about the Promised Land you have been seeking, lo these many years. The something you will find out is that the Promised Land lies in your own consciousness, and the moment you are through seeking it and begin the process of recognizing it as here and now within the secret place of your heart—that moment you see the transformation beginning to make itself manifest.

Do not expose the seed to the parching winds of human opinion. "Thou fool, do you not know that a seed must first fall into the ground and rot before it shall be made alive?" Do you not know that the seed idea must be dropped into the secret place and there lose its outer wrapping of human opinion and belief before the new manifestation shall come forth?

The ugly brown bulb is transformed into a cluster of lilies. What a transformation—all for the simple following of the law. Yet this process of change is no more wonderful than the transformation that shall go on in you, "O ye of little faith," when you can follow the law. "Be ye transformed by the renewing of your mind." How can the mind be renewed if it be not still? How can the earth be renewed unless it go deep into the secret place of the roots and there restore itself or its manifestation by the substance that is stored up there? Do you begin to see why it is that the lips shall be sealed? You who read?

The butterfly and chrysalis, the chick in the shell, and a thousand other things give you an ample idea, but all these are inadequate to convey the power of the Word that is to work out in you when you can be still.

The law states very clearly, "Ask and it shall be given you; seek and ye shall find; knock and it shall be opened unto you," and yet there be thousands who will say they have done all these things and are still without the bare necessities of life. Seeking amidst the husks of human reasoning and opinions—among the findings of the human intellect—will not be productive of much more than a grain or two of substance. Asking the world at large for freedom from your sorrows will merely bring pity or ridicule on your head. Knocking at the gates of human temples is disheartening, and yet the law continues:

> For every (no exceptions) one that asketh receiveth; and he that seeketh findeth; and to him that knocketh it shall be opened (Matt. 7:8).

The pristine beauty of this assurance sounds forth like a glorious bell across the smooth waters of a silver lake, or like an answered SOS to a tempest-tossed ship, and yet no results have come. Men have gone down in the ditch trying to wrench away from the universe just a decent living. One by one, the dreams of youth are exploded because they cannot be fulfilled, although they seemed so right and so possible of attainment.

For everyone that asketh receiveth. You may prove that you spend hours a day in good works and prayer, just as a man states, and truly, that he holds an oak tree in his hand when he shows you an acorn. In spite of the fact that you have "faith as a grain of mustard seed" that is said to be enough to move mountains, nothing happens, and nothing is going to happen until you enter the place of silence and set the seal on your lips.

When you are once in this place of silence, you find the processes reversed. Before you ask *I* will answer. The asking is merely voicing something that is about to be made visible. It is the decreeing of the thing that will eventually come into manifestation. The chick in the shell, hidden away from the world of curious, human eyes, is evolving into a new state; you will begin to see what takes place in the silence of your being and why you are commanded to "Be still, and know that I am God," and presently you leave the noisy company of those traveling in the desert and enter into your secret place, to discover that the Promised Land is not a place but a state of consciousness, and it exists in the *now* of time, the *here* of space.

> But the land, whither ye go to possess it, is a land of hills and valleys, and drinketh water of the rain of heaven; a land which the Lord thy God careth for: the eyes of the Lord thy God are

always upon it, from the beginning of the year even unto the end of the year (Deut. 11:12).

Note the words "the Lord thy God" and see if the light of the governing influence of your Christ-Consciousness does not blaze forth with such effulgence that the noonday is as the twilight, and in this revelation are revealed the glorious things that heretofore were hidden from the human mind. "Eyes have not seen ..." but it is there all the same. It makes itself manifest when the eye becomes single and when the lips become silent and when the recognition is made in the secret place. *Here* and *now* does not mean more waiting, more patience with the appearance of things; it means a beautiful transformation that goes on before your eyes, a coming into being of the Promised Land.

When you pause for a moment to consider that the Lord thy God is watching over this Promised Land, "whither ye go to possess it," from "the beginning of the year even unto the end of the year," then you can understand why you are admonished to take no thought for the body, for the food, for the purse, scrip, or upper chamber.

"I have much to say unto you, but you cannot not bear it now." No one can bear the deep Truth of Life until his lips have been sealed. No one can take the new state of consciousness until he can hold his tongue, for it is by means of the tongue—symbolically speaking—that you shall be defiled. Watch, therefore, that ye enter not into temptation to tear away the protective coating of silence from about the new idea. Let not the manifestation be retarded or deformed by your anxiety, for the moment you recognize the new idea, the soul of you is singing, no matter what the outward appearances—for anon the Child shall be born. Every idea that has its immaculate conception in the mind of silence will come forth to rule over its domain gloriously. Be still ... be still ... be still, and know that *I* am God.

The sign of a silent soul is serenity—poise and power. There is a confidence and an abandon. There is a light of joy in the consciousness.

> Serene, I fold my hands and wait ...
> —John Burroughs

Quite a different waiting from the old idea of waiting for something to happen. It is the confident waiting for the divine event to take place—a serene confidence that it is done and the mechanics will be perfectly executed. Can you see why it is necessary for you to come apart from them and be separate? Be still ... be still ... be still.

> Be silent, O all flesh, before the Lord (Zech. 2:13). For the froward is abomination to the Lord; but his secret is with the righteous Prov. 3:32).

The froward is an abomination to the Lord, the same as the one who digs up the garden after it is planted and opens the egg after it has been placed under the bird—abomination because he is destroying the manifestation that is due to appear.

"Awake, thou that sleepest, and Christ shall give thee light"—awake and arise from the dead. Fold your tent and steal silently away into the secret place where you can enlarge the borders of your tent without asking the permission of anyone. No matter how loving the advice may be, the things of Spirit that are deep and pure will have to be found alone in the silent place, alone with God.

All that is necessary to enter therein is willingness on the part of the student—willingness to listen instead of to tell, willingness to accept the promises as made by the Master and to plant the seed and let the human limitations and husks of belief rot away from it, in order that the new life may appear. In the place of the most High you have no favors to ask, no special permission to gain. What you tell yourself in secret shall be called from the housetop—the Word shall become flesh; there is a rest for the people of God. All of these beautiful things become true to the silent soul.

Be still, and know that I am God.

Chapter Seven

Breaking the Bread

Five thousand hungry men, far from food and shelter; five thousand men in the desert, hungry, calling for bread—and only five barley loaves; the nearest food depot miles away.

Dozens of empty vessels, all crying out to be filled; great, yawning, ugly, black vacuums of debt and want—and only a few drops of oil in the cruse.

Great stretches of parched desert, scorched by sun and wind—dry, barren, ugly, useless; worthless, helpless, unwanted, crying for expression—and only a small desert waterhole under a scraggy tree, half-filled with poisonous water, and a mass of bone-dry seeds buried in the sands.

Any one of these pictures is enough to make the average strong heart quail and turn away with a sense of helplessness. "Why does God permit such terrible things to exist if He is All-powerful?" "Why do I have to continue always under an avalanche of debt and limitations, with never enough to do anything with?" "Why do I lie on a bed of pain, my body racked with loathsome disease?"

"I have tried and tried and yet no results come." "Anyone could see that five loaves would not feed five thousand men. A loaf to a thousand? What good to even pause to consider such an absurd idea? What good to consider the empty jars when only a few drops of oil are visible?" Thus man reasons and thus he fails. Having drawn his conclusions in accordance with the best human understanding and wisdom, he abides by the results.

The first and great law of breaking the belief of limitation is "Judge not from appearances." We have heard it often, but we have never really *heard* it until we can do it. When you actually *hear* a word of Truth, you can fulfill it. Taking your attention away from the appearance of things, or judging not from appearances, is not merely closing the material eyes and refusing to see that which you know — in your human thinking — is real. Being "absent from the body and present with the Lord" is actually placing the attention on the invisible Source of All.

This is neither as abstract nor as difficult as it seems at first glance. It is not a difficult thing, through the process of your imagination, to possess those things which are necessary for your well-being. It is not difficult for you to imagine that it would be a simple matter to the All-Power to produce all the desires of your heart — seeing that It has already created infinitely more — right before your eyes. It is not difficult for you to place your consciousness in the realm of Spirit and there feel the freedom of the All-Spirit, being lost in the immensity of light and finding the hard outlines and forms of things all melting back into the infinite *One*—out of which all things came into being.

After all, a moment's thought will cause you to throw much of the limiting reasoning of human wisdom away. Just think of the infinite flow of water into the universe. From the single drop to the mighty torrents, where does it come from? We can, by a slow process, trace it from one stage to another back to Primal Cause. Where did it come from in the first place? What is the nature of the invisible quantity of substance which constantly repeats itself in a never-ending stream of expression and in an infinite variety of forms?

Out of the same invisible realm of substance, we see millions of different manifestations, just as out of the same garden plot we see a hundred varieties of seeds bringing forth as many different kinds of flowers and fruits, all drawing on the identical substance for their life. Why do a poppy and a grain of wheat, drawing on the same elements, bring forth such radically different manifestations? Who can answer except with the absurd reply, "It is the nature of the seed"?

Why should it seem strange, then, that man should make a conscious contact with this infinite Power and see It step up the process of time and bring out the instant manifestation of whatsoever is needed, instead of seeing it put through the limiting human thought process? Why should it be thought so absolutely outside the ken of possibility?

Further, why is it that you, the very reader of this page, will go into your garden and scatter a handful of seeds in the ground without so much as a mental effort as to how they are going to draw their substance out of the invisible? Pushing this idea back a little farther, you find it is because you have a perfect confidence that it can be done—not in a way you know but in an unseen way. Somehow or other, this tiny seed will be able to select the pigmentation of color and the qualities for its own expression. And you do not find this strange; it has ceased to be wonderful. It is natural. You dismiss it. The handful of seed is all that is necessary for you presently to reap a harvest that many men with many baskets cannot gather in.

Yet if someone said, "There are five loaves to feed five thousand hungry men," you would immediately place it under the head of miraculous—something outside the laws of nature and life. Why should it be thought more difficult to increase one substance than another? Well, you scatter your seed with abandon and with absolute faith that its increase is assured; you give it little or no thought after it is sown. But if you were to attempt to increase the loaves, you would be concerned to such an extent with the manifestation that the law would not operate.

If you have five seeds and want to increase them to five thousand, you do not lay the five seeds on the table and pray over them. You do something. You cast them into the ground. There is no wondering or questioning the action. After you have abandoned them in this way, the work on the outside is done; the next move must be from the realm of the Invisible.

When will you, you who read this page, open your eyes and see what is going on all about you? When will you start the flow of substance by taking your attention away from the symbol and placing it on the substance back of the symbol? In other words, when will you cast the seed into the ground of Spirit and let the invisible Power of the Lord work upon it? When you drop the seeds into the ground, you have already given thanks—perhaps not in words—for the harvest. You have actually accepted your good—your increase, your fulfillment—and yet you have seen nothing. But you have obeyed the law; you have not asked for a sign, knowing that the signs will follow, they do not precede.

When Jesus, the Master, saw the five thousand and the five loaves, he said to his disciples, "Give them to eat." The disciples—even as you and I— immediately looked at the problem before them and in the most intelligent manner asked, "Where can we get the bread?" Over and over, the word is spoken to us—yet the deaf ears hear nothing. When the Voice commands, it should be sufficient to cause you to move into action; for It will never say "Do," "Go," "Be," "Have," or any of the commands, unless wrapped up in that very word is the means of expressing the command in its fullness.

Strange as it may seem to the human sense, man is always in possession of enough to start the increase that will unfold or unroll until it has filled every empty thing. Hence, in the desert, five loaves were "seed" sufficient to increase the manifestation unto the need.

Jesus took the five loaves and blessed them. His blessing was one of pure recognition of the infinite increase, or the infinite abundance of substance. "He blessed ... brake ... and gave."

He disregarded absolutely all appearances; he blessed and brake and gave—and he kept on breaking the bread until everything was filled and there was enough and to spare, his attention being away from the appearance of things all the while and placed on the invisible—the very invisible out of which the tremendous increase of your seed planting took place last spring. Only his attention was so conscious of the Presence that the time lag was wiped out and it became the glowing, vibrating *Now* of Spirit.

"Borrow vessels ... not a few." The same power blessing, recognizing the infinite source of substance, looked away from the few drops of oil and began to pour it out just as it had broken the bread. And presently, out of the invisible source of all things, the flow of oil came in such abundance that everything was full to overflowing.

The only benefit of these parables is the direct application to your present manifestation. Many people stand in the place, symbolically speaking, of the Master with five thousand hungry men and five loaves or with hundreds of empty vessels and only a few drops of oil, wondering why they do not demonstrate abundance, not heeding the urge of Spirit to bless and break and give—recognize the presence of the Spirit and begin the process of breaking and giving. Wherever you are and whatever your problems may be, you have the five loaves necessary or the few drops of oil, and you can bless and break and give.

All three steps are necessary. You are doing the same thing constantly in your garden, whether consciously or unconsciously. Your garden is brought forth in just this way. You realize that half the joy of your garden is the giving of its rich harvest to others, yet many people in Truth imagine that the giving is something entirely apart from the getting. It is only by making a constant outlet for the expression of good that more can flow into your life. It is reasonable to believe that the increase of anything would stop if it had no outlet. We notice in the five loaves and five thousand men demonstration that bread was given as fast as they came for it. It was not all manifested at once and then passed out. Your substance does not have to be mountain-high before you can give it out—in fact, if the flow is not kept open, the increase stops.

It is a glorious revelation that you, just where you are, can begin the process of breaking and giving the bread of life and see the endless flow of substance making itself manifest to you and your universe.

You can begin to see why the command of "Silence" is so essential. Why, the great prayer is "Be still, and know that I am God." Not the human, limited power, but that which can step up the time lag and make the *Now* of the manifestation appear — the power which is back of this potent statement: "You say it is four months until the harvest, but I say look again." Only those that have eyes that have been opened to the reality of being can see the harvest where the human sense says planting has not yet even taken place. "Having eyes, ye see not; having ears, ye hear not." "Awake, thou that sleepest." The new dimension is edging into your picture.

Do you begin to see the futility of keeping the attention fixed on the few drops of oil or the five loaves and the hungry masses? Bring this right down to your problems, and a door will open to you. A new joy will fill you, for you will discover that you have all that is necessary to bring out the fullness of the invisible substance.

Beloved, do not let it be said of you anymore, "Ye seek me, not because ye saw the miracles, but because ye did eat of the loaves and were filled."

Don't you see how perishable is the symbol but how unlimited is that which is back of it? "Labor not for the meat which perisheth, but for that meat which endureth unto everlasting life."

Why should you worry about the symbols? Take your attention away from them or the lack of them and keep breaking and giving of the precious substance. Do not invert the process and reason thus in your hearts, "If I give I shall get." That is a losing game. Give because the *overflowing* substance within you seeks its level—that is, its complete fulfillment—automatically. You cannot help pouring out the gift of the Father when you begin to see that the infinite flow of joy is coursing through you and through your universe.

Rejoice and be exceeding glad and let fall the drenching rain of recognition of the presence of God; let it fall on the barren desert of your life, and the desert will blossom as a rose, for it has the seeds of infinite possibilities hidden away in its burning sands, awaiting recognition. It is well. Break your bread and give it to the hungry multitude of desires in your life.

Chapter Eight

Power

All power is given unto me
in heaven and in earth.

—*Matt. 28:18*

In spite of this, men still wonder if it is possible for God to set aside the evil in their lives; if it is possible for the All-Power to neutralize the fearful problems that have come to them. "All power is given unto me in heaven and in earth." This statement is certainly not true of man, for he seems strangely without power. In fact, everything else in the universe seems to have more power than man. Hence, he is subject to all sorts of influences over which he seemingly has no control. God is ruled out of His universe, and a power of evil is enthroned.

When man examines his human self to ascertain his capacities and abilities, he finds them strangely lacking in power. He takes into account his birth, breeding, education, muscular power, general health, etc., and knows exactly what he can do, even to his earning capacity. This is verified by thousands of laws, statistics, and proofs, as well as the findings of the wisdom of the world. What good is it to tell a man who has measured himself by these standards that a power exists that can and does make every one of his findings null and void?

He knows he cannot lift a two-hundred-pound weight—he has tried it. What is the good of argument on this point? He can prove it to you. Yet occasionally, he finds that someone in a moment of excitement or stress has lifted many times his own weight, and this in spite of the best findings of human intellect. He knows it cannot be done, and yet time and again, it has been done—and man says "by a supernatural power." Exactly, and that is what he should say, and that recognition should suddenly turn his attention away from the limited, human capacity unto the supernatural Power.

The law by which this power is discovered and used is by taking the attention away from the limitations of the human world and contemplating the real and supernatural universe, the unconditioned power of God.

The following was clipped from the New Yorker. It was found in an article on Zimbalist, the great violinist:

> Somehow, nobody told Zimbalist that he was supposed to play the piano, too; but during the final examinations, in his eighteenth year, they handed him a Beethoven sonata to be read at sight, in the presence of the whole facility. He had never touched a piano except to get his "A." He sat down, however, got his breath, played. When he finished, he was told to close the book and repeat the whole sonata from memory; he

did so. After a moment of silence, the room broke unanimously into applause—an unheard of demonstration.

All the human intellect in the universe could not conceive this possible. They would immediately say it could not take place, and yet it did take place. Few things could be more difficult. It bespeaks a power which is entirely outside human capacity. Imagine reading a difficult sonata once and then playing it note-perfect, and this, too, on an instrument you had never touched.

Just think about it a moment; then you will begin to see what the power of which Jesus spoke is capable of doing. It is capable of setting every human law at naught. Is it any wonder, then, that within this law lies the kingdom of heaven, and should it not thrill you to know that this very law is possible of operation within your midst?

"Ah, but Zimbalist is a genius." Not being able to dispose of the Power, which upsets the most cherished laws of the human mind, it finally disposes of the matter thus. But presently it is confronted with another interesting news item concerning an invalid who had been paralyzed for twenty years and was being conveyed on a stretcher to another town. In crossing the tracks, the carriers suddenly discovered they were in the way of an on-coming express train. Without time to go forward or backward the length of a stretcher, they did the most natural human thing. The law of self-preservation came into play, and they dropped the stretcher and fled. From the human standpoint, it was certain destruction to the invalid, who had not walked a step for years and could not move himself. But what happened? He, the invalid, suddenly seeing the train, leaped from the stretcher and ran. But how? Only a moment before, he could not move. A miracle had happened, said the press, and so it had. Something that the human mind could not conceive as possible had happened, and laws of twenty years' standing were as naught.

What about it? Do you think it is necessary for the God-Power to have an express train in the picture in order to operate? Do you think it is always necessary to have some terrific thing about to happen before God is able to come into manifestation? It does not matter whether it takes an on-rushing express train, an earthquake, or torrent to produce it, or whether you produce it in the quiet of your own soul. One thing alone is necessary, and that one all-important point is your willingness to take your attention away from the limited human concept of yourself. In the simple language of Jesus, we find that "to be absent from the body and present with the Lord" is the way of great miracles. Looking at the appearances of things only binds you to the human capacity, which is practically nil.

The story of the prophet and his servant is the story of every man. The servant, looking to appearances, saw they were about to be destroyed and called out in fear. But the prophet was smiling and called the servant's attention to the invisible-visible power and said, "Those that are for us are more than those that are against us." That is, the power that is for you is greater than all the combined beliefs opposed to you. The reward is rich if you can heed the Scriptures—"Be absent from the body and present with the Lord." If the Lord knows your every need and supplies it before you ask, then why not fix the attention on the Allness of God now?

"They that trust in the Lord shall be as Mount Zion, which cannot be removed, but abideth forever."

Can you but place your trust in the Lord, not as some mysterious power but as the very presence of Life within you and your universe, then you can know the feel of instant release from the evil of human belief. "With God all (not some) things are possible." *All* things are possible. Do you hear, you who read this book? "Believest thou this?"

"They shall not hurt nor destroy in all my holy mountain: for the earth shall be full of the knowledge of the Lord, even as the waters cover the sea."

We begin to see, then, that Jesus was a Truth-sayer when he said, "I come not to destroy, but to fulfill." The idea that we are here for the purpose of destroying something gives way to the truth of the redemption of everything. The fulfilling of the Law is the realization of the presence of the Power which is able to do that which the human limitation finds impossible.

God "is able to do for us exceeding abundantly above all that we ask or think, according to the power that worketh in us." The God-Power is able and willing to do that which completely outdistances human thinking, with its limited idea of the possibilities of the God-Power. But note: the crux of the whole thing lies in the word *according*. According to your acceptance of the God-Power as everywhere present, and as omnipotent, will It be able to do more than human thought can conceive of. The God-Power reverses every human law. "Before they call I will answer" is one of the interesting things to be considered. From the standpoint of reason, this is absolutely ridiculous; so, inversely, to the divine Mind, the reason of man is "foolishness in the eyes of God."

Can you not see, you who read this page, how we are fast approaching the state of "Be still, and know that I am God"? Can you see why the noisy chattering of the human mind must give way to the glorious peace and poise of the Presence? If your question is answered before it is asked, why repeat it over and over; why not stay on the finished idea?

> The former things have passed away. They shall not be remembered, nor will they come to mind (Isa. 65:17; 42:9).

Even the memory of the evil shall be passed through the waters of forgetfulness, and man shall arise from this glorious bath and be clothed in a cloud of perfume from an unseen flower of Spirit. He shall stand on the heights naked and be enveloped by a golden veil of life. The former things shall have passed away and shall not be remembered any more.

> The works that I do, I do not of myself; the Father that dwelleth in me, he doeth the works (see John 14:10).

Indwelling in every man is this Father, which is able to do more that we ask or think, and able to set aside the limitations of the human expression. Making your union with this Father brings you to the point of which Jesus spoke: "I can of myself do nothing," but "with God all things are possible." And a little contemplation will cause you to see that if you will open wide the doors of your consciousness and let this Christ come into your life and become one with you, "the Father within" will do the works.

"Behold, I have received commandment to bless: and he hath blessed, and I cannot reverse it." The capacity of the Father within is to bless, and the meaning of the word *bless* conveys that heavenly capacity of invoking the divine favor. It is wondrous and beautiful to contemplate that "I have received the commandment to bless." The *I* of you hath received the commandment to bless, to invoke the divine favor. It is that which sets aside the sternest human laws and beliefs; it is the power which causes the oldest and time-honored limitations to crumple as a sandcastle before a tidal wave.

Nothing can revoke this divine blessing when once it is recognized and called into manifestation. All that is necessary to bring out the glorious revelation are the simple words "I bless you," spoken from the conscious recognition of your at-one-ment with the Father within, remembering all the while that this glorious teaching is given to the child. Not the child in years, but in consciousness—the mind that can accept the fact that God is the only Power and is everywhere present.

"All power is given unto me in heaven and in earth." In the mind and in the body is all power given unto the I AM.

Arise and go forth with this glorious command written in gold across your heart: "Behold, I have received the commandment to bless (to invoke the divine Power), and he hath blessed, and I cannot reverse it." You can go your way invoking the divine Power because you are the Child of the living God, and right now and right in the place you stand, you have the power to do this.

"Arise, shine; for thy light is come, and the glory of the Lord is risen upon thee."

You are the Being of Light in the universe of Light. It is well with you *now*.

Chapter Nine

Christmas

For unto us a child is born ... and the government shall be upon his shoulder: and his name shall be called Wonderful, Counsellor, The mighty God, The everlasting Father ... And of his reign there shall be no end.

—Isa. 9: 6, 7

So beloved, to you who read this page, at this very instant great floods of spiritual light are breaking over you. The soul of you arises at the blast of the silent trumpet, and the glad tidings are proclaimed throughout your universe. The picture of history and legend that you have cherished so long in your heart has suddenly come to life, and the divine event takes place within you—within the manger of your heart. You, the poor worm of the dust, the sinner, the outcast, are actually the lowly manger wherein the Christ is born. His name is to be called Wonderful, and the government shall be upon his shoulders. The government of what? The government of your life. The poor, struggling sinner who has so long been under the law of "When I would do good, I do evil," he it is who suddenly sees the star in the East and goes towards the stable of his own heart and finds there at this glorious instant the divine event taking place.

And the government of your life is to be upon his shoulders. All the worrying and trying and effort falls away. "Cast your burden on Me, and *I* shall sustain thee … Lean on Me … Come unto Me …" A hundred invitations are given to the struggling man, but until the divine event takes place, he turns a deaf ear to it all, unable to see how it can possibly take place—the quickening of the Father within; the recognition of the divine Sonship; the glorious revelation of the at-one-ment with God. "Yet in my flesh shall I see God." All these and a hundred more testimonies hover about the new babe like angels of the Lord, enfolding the universe of the newborn in the soft folds of their wings. It is wonderful. Heaven and earth are full of Thee.

The struggle is over. "He that loseth his life … shall find it." He that loses his personal life, his life of separateness, in the immensity of the All-Life shall find the real meaning of Life; shall find the hidden manna and the living waters and shall never hunger or thirst again. If your will be lost in the divine Will or if your human governing be given over to the Christ, then your will becomes His will and His will becomes your will, and you see the new regime setting in.

The glorious heralds of the New Day go forth and proclaim it to the uttermost parts of your sin-bound universe. The prisons of thought are opened and the prisoners are set free. There is great rejoicing in the land, for you that were dead are made alive.

For unto us a child is born, and his name shall be called Wonderful. His name shall be called Wonderful. Do you hear? Do you feel it? You who read this page—you? Blessings, floods of blessings, holiness, glorious swirls of illumination are yours; the heavenly hosts are descended unto you. You are in a blaze of light, or revelation, in the glorious *now*. The soul of you at this time is singing "Glory Hallelujah, Christ is born." Not in a far-off country, not in the dead history of yesteryears, but in the glorious *now*, right in the midst of the fear-filled life. Christ is born, and the government shall be upon His shoulders. The wonder of it fills you with silence so great and powerful that you are lost in the immensity of it all.

The government shall be upon His shoulders, and it shall therefore be right and just and good. Fear not—it is well with thee. Let go of the personal striving. You are now about your Father's business, and this is the eternal expression of harmony and joy. A new sense of integrity will come to you. "Blessed shalt thou be when thou comest in, and blessed shalt thou be when thou goest out." The lazy, sluggish mind shall give place to fresh streams of activity. Like a frozen river that is suddenly touched by the hot tropic sun, the frozen river of your life shall burst forth into expression. Or like a flood that passes through the stagnant waters of life, this glorious awakening shall sweep away all the scum and stagnation of human fears and thinking and leave in its place the healthful waters of activity.

Be not anxious. The government shall be upon His shoulders, and it will be well with thee. Fear not.

"All the ends of the earth" shall come, the ends of your universe. They shall hear of the new birth and shall arise, and the kings shall come and lay their crowns and jewels at the feet of the new babe. The realms of human power, of human thinking, shall finally bend their knees to the new king.

Thus will the monarchs of Health, Wealth, and Happiness, who have been so difficult to appease, come and lay their power down. No more shall they have dominion over you, for your life shall be governed from now on, not by a group of tyrants doling out a little happiness, health, and substance to you, but by the great central Power of all—the Christ in the midst of you, and "all flesh shall see it together: for the mouth of the Lord hath spoken it." Rejoice and be exceeding glad, for your Redeemer draweth nigh. The limited concept of life shall be swept away. In place thereof is the Christ, who says, "Before you ask I will answer," instead of the tyrants of human thinking who required sacrifice of blood and fire before they could be moved to do ever so little for you.

"And he said unto me, My grace is sufficient for thee: for my strength is made perfect in weakness." When in your weakness, when in the recognition of your inability to accomplish the good you would, you come to the point of recognition of the Christ within, then you are no more "under the law but under grace." No more under the law of what? The law of your human belief; the law of your human concept of Life which was full of so much trouble; no more under the law of "When I would do good, I do evil."

"My grace is sufficient for thee." My grace, My divine influence, shall be sufficient for thee. The influence of the Divine surrounds you—it is above the possibility of failure or fear or harm. No wonder, then, that you are thrilling with joy. The long years of bondage are ended. The scorching path in the desert has terminated. You have come to the promised land.

"My grace is sufficient for thee." Where is the *My* of this promise and where is the *thee*? Do you not see how it all goes back to the Christmas, to the new birth of that which is wonderful and upon whose shoulders the government shall rest? The government of the human personality shall be upon the Christ, and the grace of the Christ shall be sufficient for the human manifestation.

Sufficient is enough. Do you hear, you who read this page—you? "My grace is sufficient for thee." Sufficient is enough. Over and over, this revelation comes to mankind, and at last, out of it he perceives the wonders of the divine Influence. The divine Influence is that which causes the acorn to press its tiny shoot through the hard earth and even through places and under conditions that are pronounced hopeless. This same divine Influence is that which enables you to pass by safely. It is that which opens the doors in walls that otherwise appear blank and adamant.

This glorious quality of the divine Influence which we call grace resides in the consciousness of the Christ-Mind, and it is this very Christ-Mind that you were told to "let" be in you. Let the Child be born—in other words, when we have the Christmas celebration within our own souls, then the Christ is born within us; then we begin to experience the law of Grace, or the divine Influence. We begin to see the old beliefs fall away. We begin to see that the legends of Father Christmas and the Christmas tree are truths told so that the uninitiate should not despoil them of their precious substance. They are the pearls which are not cast before swine.

The Christmas tree is only another way of expressing the tree of life that lies in the midst of the garden and upon whose branches are all good gifts, the gifts of Spirit. Whosoever heareth the Word will henceforth not be a beggar for the gifts of life but will go within his own garden and take his own gifts. All that the Father hath is thine. When the law of Grace is set free, the law of limitation is made null and void. You will find then that the promise "Before they call I will answer" is something true and wonderful.

You are your own Christmas tree and your own Father Christmas. You are the center and circumference of your being. You stand in the center of your universe and at the uttermost point of your universe. Spirit is All, and only when man accepts his birthright and goes forward upon these new lines can he possibly know the joy and thrill that the truth about Christmas brings.

When you realize for an instant, "For unto us a child is born ... and his name shall be called Wonderful, Counseller, The mighty God, The everlasting Father ... and upon his shoulders shall be the government," then you have taken Christmas out of the symbolism and gotten back to the soul of it. It ceases to be a day of gifts, with pudding and turkey—and a possible church service thrown in with a magnanimous prayer for the poor—and turns itself into a heavenly recognition of the Presence: flings wide the portals of a *new* year, a *new* life, and a *new* field of attainment.

At the name of Christ, every knee shall bend. At the nature, or name, of the Christ, the knee of every human belief shall bend to do Him homage. Every so-called power shall bend before the *one* and *only* Power, who rules by grace. "My grace is sufficient for thee." It is wonderful.

> Joy to the world (your world), the Lord is come! Let earth receive her King (Isaac Watts).

Joy to your world—joy to your world—the Lord hath come. Lord of Lords and King of Kings is born within you, born within your consciousness. Lord of lords and King of kings, and besides this there is no other. Not a little personal despot of a king but a glorious consciousness that is one with the universal God.

Everything is fused with the new-old idea, the birth of the Christ within you. You are filled with light and the radiance of the New Day.

Awake!—with the new birth, man loses his fantastic idea of demonstrating God and lets God demonstrate him; lets the Light reveal the answer which was before the question; sees the futility of demonstrating a thing which immediately disintegrates, and returns to the endless Source from which it pours.

Chapter Ten

The Years that the Locust Hath Eaten

I will restore to you the years
that the locust hath eaten.

—*Joel* 2:25

A meaningless bit of Bible language, a scrap of Oriental poetry, and yet hidden away therein is a secret and a promise so wonderful that it makes the interest in life flare up into reality again.

The years that the locust hath eaten are the years that are wasted. So many have found themselves looking backward over a life of fruitless years — years of struggle; years consumed with futility and despair; years filled with unexpressed dreams and ambitions; ugly years of vacuity and nothingness. Hundreds of people have spent ages trying to bring out the higher consciousness, only to arrive at a place of disappointment. Old, worn-out bodies and insufficient funds seem to have been the reward for their years of labor. The locust of human thought has eaten up all that was worthwhile and left but the ghastly skeletons.

Many of these fall back on the old, hateful teaching that when they "sleep" they shall waken to a new and wonderful state of things. They only accept this because they have failed to bring out the

Presence here and now. The bitterness of failure is upon them.

> Behold, I show you a mystery: We shall not all die, but we shall be changed … in the twinkling of an eye, at the last trump … the dead (in Christ) shall be raised … and we (the living) will be changed (1 Cor. 15:52).

The last trump that is to sound, which will change you, or raise you from the mass of dead beliefs, is not a noise that shall be heard with the human ear. It is "the still small voice" of the Master, who standeth at the door and knocks. It is this very silent-audible voice which will awaken the dead and change the living, and it is this glorious power that will suddenly cause you to know that the "years which the locust hath eaten" are restored and that it is not too late; it is not just a whitewashing of rotten timbers but a newness, a restoration of the temple that was almost destroyed.

"Destroy this temple (body) and in three days I will raise it up." "I have power to pick it up or lay it down." We are speaking of the temple of the body, which is the "temple of the living God" and is therefore a temple of perfection. We are speaking of the temple of life which, through belief, has been consumed with the locust of human thought. Yea, these very temples that we call human bodies—these same bodies that we have called vile and have begged to be delivered from—these shall be restored.

The day of platitudes is over for the one who has heard the voice of the inner Lord. He is no longer trying to make his old body over by repeating a lot of words or ideas. He knows he must be born again—he must start all new and fresh. He must give up his temporal power and become the new, fresh babe of Spirit.

"Ye must be born again." Old Nicodemus, when told that he must be born again, put up the same argument that you and I put forth when we are first initiated into the inner courts and hear the wonders that must be made manifest. No wonder—we have seen so much failure and such tiresome years of earnest effort being consumed by the locusts of failure and futility.

"He restoreth my soul." The substance wasted in prodigality is restored in all its freshness. The prodigality may not necessarily have been sin in the terms of what the world calls sin, but it may have been spent in a thousand and one ways that proved futile and availed you nothing.

"Return unto the Lord, and he shall forgive your backsliding." We are just beginning to understand that through a mistaken belief of life in the body we have wasted our substance, and we have nothing but the locust-eaten years to look upon.

"Behold, I make all things new." Do you believe? You, who read this line? Where do you locate the *I* of which you speak? Can you see—you who read these lines—that the new day is slowly but surely

dawning and the words of the Spirit of Truth, whoever spoken through, are being fulfilled?

"I shall restore the years that the locust hath eaten."

"Yet in my flesh shall I see God." Do you believe
this, you who are reading? Do you think it is possible, and do you stop to think what it will be like to
see God in your flesh? In my flesh shall I see God.
What would you see if you saw God in your flesh?
Think it over—certainly you would not see the years
that the locust hath eaten.

"His flesh shall be fresher than a child's; he shall
return to the days of his youth."

The human mind cannot grasp this. It comes
under the head of the seeming impossible; therefore,
it comes under the scope of the I AM Consciousness—
the doer of the impossible. Note the word *fresher*.
Why fresher? Because it is the spiritualized flesh. In
my flesh shall I see God. In my flesh shall I see Spirit
materialized. We know Jesus raised his body from
the death of materiality and from the material
limitations, and yet he had a body which could be
touched and handled. But it was fresher even than
the body of a child, or the flesh of a child, because it
had lost all earthliness and had become pure Spirit.
These are the deep things of Spirit. My words are
spirit, and they are truth, and "they shall not return
unto me void."

Do you hear, you who read? The deep and
hidden things are being revealed to you. "Be still,
and know that I am God." This means the human

laws of birth, growth, maturity, and decay are no more operative for you. You are the risen Lord. The Spirit has become flesh, and the years that have been eaten by the locust are restored. They are revealed in all their beauty, and nothing is lost or found wanting.

"The kingdom of heaven has come nigh unto you." Secretly, we are seeing, through the mass of words, the power behind them and are leaving the symbols for the reality. In the seed is stored up all the plant will need to express itself in perfection. Lost in the Life of God, you are finding that the substance spent in riotous living is restored to you.

Do you not see that when you lose your life— the human sense of birth, growth, maturity, and decay—you will find the eternal Life, that which will restore all which you thought was eaten by the locust—human belief? "For this *is* (present tense) life eternal, that they might know thee."

Beloved, the day breaks; gradually we shall know the truth of the statement "And God shall wipe away all tears ... there shall be no more crying." The belief of human misery shall pass away, and you shall stand revealed—the Son of the living God.

> Thou shalt forget thy misery, and remember it as waters that pass away (Job 11:16).

The hour has struck. The door is closed. We are beginning the process from within out, which shall change us, or reveal to us the "full stature of Christ." "Eyes have not seen"—we do not look for a pattern or model of this temple of the living God, but we gaze inwardly to the picture "shown us upon the mount," and this is the picture that shall be reproduced in the flesh. "Yet in my (my own) flesh shall I see God." Do you hear, you who read? "Believest thou this?"

"You say it is four months until the harvest. I say, look again." Suddenly there is a telescoping of time. Time is mental; so is weight. This ability to telescope the illusion is a capacity which you possess—in other words, returning to the Father, a blending with the One where *two* does not exist, but "before you ask" is the Law.

Chapter Eleven

The Lord Said unto My Lord

The Lord said unto my Lord, Sit thou on my right hand, till I make thine enemies thy footstool.
                                                        —Ps. 110:1

The Universal Consciousness speaks to Its manifestation. The Son becomes one with the Father as Jesus stated. "I and my Father are one." "My Father is greater than I." So man is beginning to see and to recognize the fact that the I AM within him is the Father-Consciousness which, by man's acceptance, becomes one with the Whole. All ideas of separation are swept away in the glorious manifestation of Light. All fear and limitation are made null and void. Instantly you see that the Lord, the inner Lord, who has become lost in the maze of the belief-world and is almost overcome with the seeming enemies, has to put up his sword and "see the salvation of the Lord." What Lord?

"Until I make thine enemies thy footstool." When there ceases to be retaliation, when man ceases to fight back but steps aside, as it were, the "vengeance is mine" is perfectly worked out into expression in a way man knows not of. His enemies have reaped the whirlwind. Whosoever tries to steady the ark of another finds his arm withered away.

If a man throws a rubber ball at a brick wall, it returns to him of its own volition, but if there happens to be a hole in the wall, it goes through and does not return. So is it with evil. If thy enemies throw evil at you and you accept it, then you have to pay the ugly penalty of getting rid of that which you have accepted. You then set about to get even with your adversary, and the result is discord and possibly destruction for both of you. But if you have no hole in the wall—that is, if you refuse to accept the evil— it returns with accelerated force to its sender. You do not have to seek revenge. "Vengeance is mine, saith the Lord"—the reaction of evil is its own punishment and cure. You have no enemies except those you accept as such within your own consciousness.

Judging from appearances and looking to people as detached, separate beings causes you to manifest dissension, strife, and evil. "Know ye not that ye are gods" has been interpreted to mean that a personality can rise up and make itself as a god, instead of realizing you are a god in capacity as soon as you recognize you have within you the I AM Consciousness, which has instant power to contact the universal Lord and to call into manifestation unlimited and unconditioned power.

Nothing shall by any means hurt you (Luke 10:19).

This is the statement of the mind that realizes its at-one-ment with the universal Power. When the

inner Lord of you listens for and makes its contact
with the Lord, nothing (not anything) can hurt you,
for you can instantly call into manifestation legions
of angels. You have but to put up your sword and
see the salvation of the Lord—this Lord of lords who
is not in any way subject to what you think or what
anyone else thinks; who acts independently of all
thought; that which doeth the things impossible to
human law.

"Ye shall eat your own words." That which you
send out in the way of judgment comes back to you
eventually with accelerated force and from the least
expected place. Thus is the law of the Cosmic Force.
Little by little, we are learning the protection in the
command "Judge not, lest ye be judged" and are
beginning the process of seeing only that which is
good. After all, the truth of the adage "Set a thief to
catch a thief" is not so far wrong when it comes to
many other things that we see in the world.

Be not afraid of the truth. Welcome with open
arms anything that will clear away the debris of human
thinking, no matter how time-honored it may be.

The quaking fear of the servant gives place to
confidence when you realize the presence of the
inner Lord. He is above all fear, limitation, and lack.
Nothing can by any means hurt you when you recognize this fact, and "though ten thousand fall at thy
right hand, it shall not come nigh thee" unless you
open unto it and accept it, and then it becomes real
to you.

"Agree with thine adversary quickly whilst thou art in the way." We do not fight or argue with the adversary. Your refusing to accept the evil is silent and is not done in a whirlwind of denial or argument. Your adversary will become your footstool—that is, he shall be placed under the dominion of the Christ within you and shall be as nothing the moment you step aside and let the Lord, the great Cosmic Power of the universe, return the evil which you did not accept.

Once you have accepted a condition or thing, it is yours, and you will fight *all night* with it, until further light comes and causes you to let go. Finally, you will have to *loose it and let it go.* Then why accept it at all—however real it seems, however unjust or hateful? Just close the door of the mind to it, and the universal Mind against which it has struck will return it to its proper place of manifestation.

That is why Jesus was so fearless. He refused to accept evil as real. He left the penalties to the Power of the Universal, to the Power of the God of Love. In reality, God does not hurt or harm any in all His kingdom. One would not blame a door that was blown open by a violent wind for injuring a man who was standing in the way thereof. Obviously the door did nothing. You strike yourself when you strike another, and rather sharply too, provided that other refuses to accept the blow. What you know of evil for another you know for yourself, more especially if that other happens to know the law of non-acceptance. Watch, take care you enter not into temptation. "Vengeance is mine" is a terrible law to set in operation. You are the only one who can set it in operation against yourself, and it is possible only by trying to injure another. "Judge not" is a hard, fast law, and there is no (not any) loophole for your superfine judgment to get through. Watch ... watch ... watch that ye enter not into temptation.

When this idea first came to me, it was so terrible and overpowering that I had a feeling of despair. I knew that so much judgment had already gone out into the universe. True, much of it I thought I was entitled to make—but here was a hard, fast truth that could not be compromised.

I realized that enemies were merely thoughts since one man's meat could be another's poison, and one man's enemy could be another's savior.

I saw clearly how the God of Love could be, and was, the God of vengeance; how the wrath of God was quite natural and just. I saw that the universal Mind merely threw back to us that which we put into it, whether it be good, bad, or indifferent thinking—that our life was composed of all this. I was in despair, and most everybody I knew was in the same boat. And then the command:

> The Lord said unto my Lord, sit thou at my right hand until I make thine enemies thy footstool (Ps. 110:1).

Gradually I began to see that these evil thoughts I had sent out were my enemies, and if they had not been accepted by those to whom I had directed them and were coming back to me, I too would refuse to accept them, and when they hit against the closed door of my consciousness, they would be dashed to pieces since they had made the complete circle and found no lodging. So in reality, I could free myself from the ugly kickback of my own wrong thinking, whether done recently or years ago. I would sit by and see my enemies, my evil thoughts—whether expressed or unexpressed, whether new or old—made as my footstool; that is, put into subjection, redeemed; dashed to pieces like evil birds that have rushed headlong against the thick glass of a lighthouse.

Yes, there was not only a sudden freedom for those whom I had judged evilly, but there was also a freedom for myself from the ugly reaction of these thoughts that needs must come out of the universal Mind. No matter what the evil had been or was, no matter how deep you had sunk into the mire of belief, repentance—refusal to participate further in the hideous game of seeing evil in another—would bring about freedom from the manifestation of evil thinking and action.

"Believe on the Lord Jesus Christ, and thou shalt be saved." There is no ambiguity about it. This utter casting yourself on the inner Lord and listening for the voice of the Universal Consciousness will cancel all the karmic debts and fears, whether prenatal or present.

The moment the Magdalene came to this point of recognition, she heard the voice saying, "Neither do I condemn thee—go and sin no more." This voice of the Lord speaking to her Lord was making her enemies as naught. She could not find one among all of them who could accuse her, because she had suddenly become one with the Father, and He found nothing to condemn.

This is a wonderful example of the working of the infinite Mind and is the door of release for thousands of earnest souls. From a human standpoint, I suppose, there were many in the crowd about the woman who could have testified to certain things that they knew about her, but suddenly this oneness with the Spirit made it impossible for those things to be anything but disintegrating beliefs. You see "I have a way that ye (man of the world) know not of." It is the complete and perfect cancellation here and now by repentance. "Repent and be saved."

No state is impossible. No state of mind is too low or too high to receive this glorious freedom of the Sons of God. Even the thief on the cross had his chance to experience the kingdom of heaven *here* and *now*. "This day shalt thou be with me in paradise." The instant you make this repentance and refuse to accept the evil by virtue of its nothingness, then the cancellation takes place. "The Lord said unto my Lord, sit thou at my right hand until I make thine enemies thy footstool." A great inrush of glory and light comes to you. A new door is opening—you are being freed, not only from the evils that have seemed to be directed at you from the outside but from the reflex action of your own evil deeds.

Does this seem right? Can a man be evil and then not pay the price? "As in Adam all die, even so in Christ shall all be made alive." When a man makes his alignment with the inner Lord and waits for "the still small voice," instead of accepting evil and then trying to dispose of it or going into the ditch because of his inability to cope with the reaction to his evil thoughts, then suddenly his past is wiped out. That which is scarlet shall be white as snow. We find the woman, with a history of all sorts of evil, suddenly made clean and free. How? By this very repentance, this very coming into the Spirit of Life.

"The Lord said to my Lord, sit thou at my right hand until I make thine enemies thy footstool." The Lord said to my Lord. The Lord says to your Lord exactly what the world is going to say because it can find no guile in you. The world that had accused the woman suddenly found it impossible to accuse her. Why? Because the Lord did not accuse her. "Neither do I condemn thee." Just ponder that glorious statement and what follows it. The whole debt was wiped out—it was made nil. It was nothing, but it was the degree of absolution. "Go and sin no more." Do not imagine that you can seek refuge from your evil thoughts and ways and expect to continue in them. The evil that is forsaken is forgiven, and the person is freed.

"The wicked shall be turned into hell." We have all experienced the hell into which we have cast ourselves because of the acceptance of evil in one form or another, but even that is not a hopeless state; for just so soon as you recognize the fact that "if you make your bed in hell, there am *I*," then do you transmute the belief.

Do you not see the glorious salvation that is offered through the Christ and how it is that "Nothing shall by any means hurt you," neither make thee afraid? You are beginning to understand how it is that evil must first be accepted before it can be manifested in your universe.

Many will argue, "Yes, but I never did anything to that person." It makes no difference. God is no respecter of persons. The universal Power that is throwing back that which you have thrown out has ways and means you know not of.

Watch … watch … watch. Repent and be saved. This is not an emotional exercise. It is just a new-borning—a new awakening into the God-world with a glorious feeling that the waters of Spirit are washing away all that has gone before. "The former things shall not be remembered nor come into mind." They shall have passed away into oblivion. It is glorious; it is glorious and wonderful. "Praise God from whom all blessings flow."

Then do the sons of God leap up with new life: "You do not need to fight … set yourselves … and see the salvation of the Lord." You can understand now what it is that makes this possible: "The Lord said to my Lord." The recognition of your oneness with the Lord of lords and King of kings makes you a majority, and the cancellation of sin takes place. It is wonderful, and more wonderful since it means the cancellation of the old debts and unsettled accounts for the past acts and thoughts.

"How shall we escape, if we neglect so great a salvation?" How, indeed, shall we escape if we have to go on fighting—even with the best methods given to us through the study of metaphysics—an endless stream of evil which is manifesting from all sorts of causes set into action and long since forgotten by us? Acts and thoughts in this and other lives that seem to be wholly apart from the control of anyone.

"How shall we escape if we neglect so great a salvation?" How indeed? "Come unto me, all ye that labor and are heavy laden." This is not spoken so much to the physically tired or the physically heavy laden, but to the souls that are burdened with false beliefs and endless meeting of evil in one form or another, most of which they are willing to admit is the result of their own thinking. What hope is there when man thinks himself to be under so ghastly a law as "When I would do good, then I do evil"? And what constant stream of evil manifestation must take place in his world? But remember that complete and whole salvation awaits the one who forsakes the evil beliefs of life and turns to God with his whole soul. He is saved from the terrible effects of his evil thinking.

"That which is told in secret is called from the housetops." That which is told in secret is what "the Lord said to my Lord." And what the Lord says to my Lord, the world at large must say to me. The Lord is saying wonderful things. "This is my beloved Son, in whom I am well pleased," is but one of them. "Be still, and know that I am God." *I* come as a great flood of waters covering the whole earth of your human thinking, and when the floods have subsided, then the ground is washed clean of the evil manifestation or that which was causing it.

"To speak no evil nor to listen to." Many will speak no evil but will listen to and think evil and then wonder why, having been apparently so good, they meet with so much evil.

"There is more rejoicing in heaven over one sinner that repenteth than over many righteous." There will be rejoicing over you, and you will hear the glorious words, "Thy sins are forgiven thee," and feel the cleansing floods of Spirit pass over you and wash you free from the evil effects of your present or former thinking and judging.

When the God-Power forgives sins, there is a total cancellation of the sin and all its effects. Man imagines he forgives sins by holding the injustice done to him against a person for the rest of his life, although he may say he has no hatred or resentment; but as long as he remembers the fault, he has not forgiven. Sin that is forgiven by God, by the Lord, is completely wiped out, just as disease that is cured is completely destroyed and its manifestation obliterated.

"Why cast ye lots for part of the garment of truth?" might well have been asked. The whole garment, the seamless robe of Christ, is thrown over you as a great panoply of light, and you are created anew, revealed as new.

The attitude, then, of the awakened Soul is not that of trying to instruct the Divine but one of listening and one which says, "Speak, Lord; for thy servant heareth." And the constant prayer of such a one is, "Be Thou expressed in me."

"Be still, and know that I am God." When you are through with accepting evil of any sort, no matter what the appearances are, then you are ready to hear what "the Lord said unto my Lord." You can hear something that all the prayers of the human universe cannot bring to pass—remembering that thy enemies are all the beliefs of inharmony that have been so real to you and have harassed you, lo these many years. A day dawns—a new day dawns. "Arise and shine, for thy light has come and the glory of God has risen upon thee."

The price has already been paid for eternal Life for you; but you will still die in spite of the entreaty "Why will ye die?" until you accept the gift of Life eternal. No life can be eternal that is sin-filled, and by sin-filled I mean filled with evil thoughts for yourself or another or the world at large. But the gift of Life eternal is given unto all those who believe. "I have a way ye know not of."

"I am the way—walk ye in it."

"Verily I say unto you: Whatsoever ye shall bind on earth shall be bound in heaven; and whatsoever ye shall loose on earth shall be loosed in heaven."

"He that loseth his life for my sake shall find it." Do you not see, then, that if you bind evil on the earth, it shall be bound in your consciousness and will constantly reproduce itself? If you bind evil on another, you bind it to yourself like holding a poisonous asp to your breast. And inversely speaking, what you loose on earth shall be loosed in heaven. If you loose the brother that you have held captive and a prisoner to your opinions and beliefs, ye shall also be loosed—set free. It is wonderful.

Watch ... watch ... watch. What are you going to accept? When are you going to sit in the quiet place and listen for the still small voice? "The Lord said unto my Lord" When are you going to get the glorious revelation of the Lord, the universal Mind speaking to the individual point of expression. "Be still, and know that I am God."

"Fear thou not; for I am with thee: be not dismayed; for I am thy God ... I will help thee; I will uphold thee with the right hand of my righteousness." Be not dismayed; *I* have a way you know not of, of wiping out the evil and making your enemies as your footstool.

I am the Truth, *I* do not use it. It emanates from Me through the five senses and extends them into Reality.

Come unto Me, and I will give you rest …
the Lord said to my Lord.

Chapter Twelve

Living Waters

Running water never tires.

"For my people have committed two evils; they have forsaken me the fountain of living waters, and hewed them out cisterns, broken cisterns, that can hold no water" (Jer. 2:13).

In this little verse lies hidden the reason for most of the difficulties of the human race. "My people," you and I, have forsaken the "fountain of living waters" and made cisterns of our own—broken cisterns. We have wandered far from the living fountain, into the parched and dried desert of human experiences, and have stopped on some oasis and dug us wells and made us cisterns, trying to husband the waters of human understanding, hoping thereby to quench our thirst. But the cisterns are broken and the water does not satisfy us. The prodigal is far removed from his father's house, and yet he is as near to it as he will ever be. Everything that is real and eternal is here and now, and the "Open sesame" is *recognition*.

The prodigal has been feeding and watering the outward body and has not been satisfied. His state goes from bad to worse. And the prodigal is the story of every man. The dead letter of the word sticks in his throat. He knows that his fathers did eat bread in the wilderness and are dead. He has come to the end of the human satisfaction. The broken cistern is dry; the stagnant waters of human reasoning are unfit to quench the appalling thirst.

It is then, perhaps, that he heeds the admonition of the Voice: "Turn ye even unto me with all your heart" and "ye shall find rest for your souls." It is an invitation that is many times passed by because of the human argument: "What? Am I fit to enter the rest of the righteous? I, who have left undone so many things that should have been done, and have done so many things that should not have been done?" But there is a beautiful insistence on the request, "Turn ye even unto me," for "my ways are not your ways."

The ways of the *Me* of Spirit are not the ways of the prodigal, who has spent his substance in riotous living. The ways of Spirit are not the ways of the human reasoning and wisdom; for "as the heavens are high above the earth, so are my ways higher than your ways." So what use for you to hold out any longer with your human understanding and reasoning? "My ways are past finding out." No man can put the ways of God on a laboratory table and dissect them to find out how they can set aside the human laws.

What if ten thousand people have gone down by the false law? It shall not come nigh you (provided you have "turned even unto me with all your heart"). What if, ever since the beginning of time, a human law has worked out successfully? There is always the exception, and that is the time that the God-Power is brought into play and the poor, puny, human intellect rears its great head of wisdom and says, "A miracle has happened," a "supernatural law." Exactly—a miracle to the human sense but a natural functioning of the God-law.

Incurable, impossible, hopeless, improbable are all words in the dictionary of man—they find no place in the courts of the Lord. The unconditioned power of God asks no permission of the race of human thought to set aside one of its laws. The sternest, most hard and fast law of the human wisdom is less than a bit of thistledown battering against the walls of China. There is no recognition of the existence of a false law that has to be set aside. There is a simple, natural expression of the God-law—the eternal harmony of itself—and when this expresses and destroys the belief-law, man says, "A miracle has happened."

Feeding upon the letter, which is dead, is no way to attain Life everlasting. Drinking the stagnant waters of the history of evil is no way to quench the thirst of the soul.

Gradually we are beginning to see that "Man shall not live by bread alone, but by every word that proceedeth out of the mouth of God." He is gradually sensing the fact that drinking of living waters and eating hidden manna is not such an imaginary thing as it was formerly thought to be.

"Ye have bread that they know not of." The awakened soul is beginning to know that he, being a spiritual being in a universe of Spirit, must be, and is, perfectly sustained in this medium of expression. He knows that the spiritual man must be fed with Spirit and watered by the living waters. He then sees more into the command, "Be absent from the body and present with the Lord." He begins experiencing the feel: "I am a spiritual being in a spiritual universe," and he takes his attention away from the physical manifestation and begins to literally feed on the Spirit. His body is beautifully fed and watered—he laves in the River of Life and is beginning to be impressed with the consciousness that if he eats this food and drinks this water, he shall never hunger and thirst again.

"Never"—think this over. The statement is "never." "Hold fast to that which is good." If you, on the invisible side or in the pure light of Spirit, partake of this food and drink these living waters, you shall never hunger or thirst again. Never. What about the human body, then, never being in want of food or drink again? Do you see what lies hidden in this wonderful revelation? Do you begin to see that "the Word became flesh" and "In my flesh shall I see God"—right into manifestation? Can you understand that to feed and water yourself in the pure essence of Spirit, not regarding or looking for the manifestation, will cause your physical body to be properly fed and watered? It is wonderful.

You shall also find that conceiving yourself as the being of Spirit, in the universe of pure Spirit, eating the food and drinking the living waters of Spirit, the physical body will take on a finer tone. "Yet in my flesh shall I see God." The soul and body of man will become one, even as Jesus and Christ became one; and all the glorious revelations of the Spirit—"searching the joints and marrow," the "Word becoming flesh," and "yet in my flesh shall I see God"—shall be made true to you. Your body shall be a well-watered garden, a glorious garden; the desert of your body shall blossom as a rose.

You who read this page, do you begin to see the new idea? Do you begin to understand that what you do on the invisible in the sacredness of Truth and the Christ-Consciousness shall diffuse Its shadow of expression through the material universe and make all things new?

"Eat my body, drink my blood" is more than a bit of poetry. Relax and let go; conceive yourself in the glowing, white light of Spirit and partake of the holy meal; "eat" the body of Christ Jesus, the substance of Life, and drink the blood of inspiration that transcends all reason and human understanding and belief.

You are the being of Light, in a universe of Light, and you shall clothe yourself in garments of Light and of Praise—yes, literally, in the glowing silence you shall clothe yourself in the garments of Light, the garments of Praise, the garments of

Thanksgiving, and verily ye shall be clothed on the human plane. Fear not!

You go forward on the way of inspiration. The eyes of Spirit are now made flesh, and the former statement, "Having eyes ye see not, and ears ye hear not," is no more true for the human eyes of flesh— into these very eyes the Spirit has come. The Spirit shall be flesh, and naturally the limitations of the human, material vision fade away with the increase of a wondrous sense of Light, and you see and hear and know "what is the height and depth and breadth."

Limitations that were true and were laws to the human sense of sight are no more true. "Yet in my flesh shall I see God." "Believest thou this," you who read this page? If so, then can you not see that when you partake of the spiritual food in a conscious way, your physical body will be beautifully cared for?

"The bread which cometh down from heaven"— where is heaven? What is heaven? Where is the *Me*? The only place you can contact God is within your own consciousness. So you are very near to the glorious revelation of the being of pure Spirit. "Behold, I stand at the door and knock … if any man will open unto me, I will come in to him, and will sup with him, and he with me." The very coming in to sup with you means the perfect union of soul and body. The body shall be permeated with the Spirit and shall manifest the joys of the kingdom of heaven here and now.

Can you not see that when you bring together the soul and body you cannot want again for anything, for all things are found within the soul of you? "I am that bread of life." "If any man will eat thereof he shall never die."

"Be not afraid, only believe." All we need is a wholesome acceptance of the fact that there is a God in the universe — All-Present and willing and able to make Himself manifest in any situation or at any time. Only believe — such a wonderful restfulness after the long journey through the barren wastes of human reasoning and understanding — such a well of water to the parched lips. It is wonderful.

Go thy way. "Provide neither gold, nor silver, nor brass in your purse, nor scrip for your journey; neither two coats, neither shoes, nor yet staves; for the workman is worthy of his hire." This is the rankest kind of philosophy to the human mind, and yet so beautifully true to the one who knows that he has the living waters and the life-giving bread always within him, and that he is clothed in the garments of Light and Praise and Thanksgiving. Why should he take thought of the purse, the scrip, the journey?

What ye therefore do in silence ye shall manifest in the open courts of the world. See that ye be well fed with Spirit and clothed and watered with the life-giving essence of being.

See that ye make the journey in Spirit first, and then "the Father worketh hitherto, and I work" shall be true. The invisible Consciousness shall have perfected it before the body has yet expressed it. So is it true, "I go before you and make straight the way"; so before you go on the journey, the Father-Consciousness has gone before you and made straight the way, and you come along later and express the mechanics of the trip. "My Father" —*My Father*— "worketh hitherto, and I work" —that is, *I* carry it out into expression, and it will be perfect and complete in every detail. Remember that the Power which knows the "number of hairs of your head" and "cares for the sparrows" has fully taken care of every detail of the journey. Nothing is too small for this glorious power, nothing too large. It is wonderful. "Fear not, it is I." "Fear not, I am with you always." "I will never leave you." *I*, the center and circumference of all Being, am with you always.

If you, then, would pause in the fury of human thinking and return to your Father's house (consciousness) and partake of the invisible meal and clothe yourself with the invisible garments of Light and Praise, the starving body would go through the mechanics of eating and be perfectly satisfied. So may you carry the idea right down the line of human wants, until your soul shall magnify the Lord, the Giver of All Good, whose arm is not shortened.

Before this book was put down on paper, it existed in its entirety in the invisible. "I go before you and make straight the way."

I thank thee, O Father, Lord of heaven and earth, that thou hast hid these things from the wise and prudent, and hast revealed them unto babes (Matt. 11:25).

If this be true, why waste any more time trying to make the "wise and prudent" drink the living waters or eat the bread of life? But see to it that from this day forth you are fed and sustained on the invisible manna that cometh down from heaven.

Chapter Thirteen

The New Day

My ways are not your ways.

—*Isa. 55:8*

A balloon that seeks a higher level must of necessity throw out ballast. Just as soon as ballast is thrown overboard, the balloon automatically ascends to a new level. Suppose the balloon to be caught in a level of air charged with poisonous gas or the belt of a terrific storm? All these environmental laws operate upon the passengers, and while they may fortify themselves with gas masks and other protective aids, yet they are never for one instant out of the danger of being overcome by them. The way of complete escape for the balloon and its passengers is to throw out ballast. The moment this is done, the balloon automatically ascends to a new level, and it and its passengers operate in an entirely new environment.

This little illustration gives an adequate idea of what takes place in man when he begins to realize the truth of his Christ-Consciousness. He begins to throw out ballast—that is, certain areas of evil thinking are done away with, and he rises to an environment where the laws formerly affecting him have power no longer. He begins to see the extent to which this ascension can take place in his life. The great statement "If ye be led of the Spirit, ye are not under the law" — of your belief — is ever at the heights, and all he has to do is to release the evil beliefs he had accepted and to ascend. "Come up higher" is the call of Spirit.

The little leaven that leaveneth the whole is brought into active manifestation by the process of recognition. As soon as we begin to recognize the Christ-Self and to accept the wonders of the new life "lost in Christ," we immediately begin to see new capacities built in our consciousness. We see through the fog of human understanding and begin to perceive the reality of the perfect man.

As in the case of the balloon rising automatically to a new level, so man, when he recognizes his true Self and accepts the laws of Spirit as the only laws, automatically arrives at his new place of expression. The old idea of trying to make a new place and attempting to make things happen through struggle and fighting gives way to the glorious fact that the moment man recognizes the presence of Christ, he automatically rises to a new level of expression, and that which was true and operative in his life before now ceases to have any power over him. "The prince of this world (the world you have left, the world of belief regarding anything) comes and finds nothing in you."

Suppose you had believed sickness to be an inescapable law; you were then subject to the personal and the race consciousness regarding it; and every time the prince of the world, or the realm of sickness, came to you, you would answer back, "Here am I—speak, for Thy servant heareth." The manifestation would automatically take place, and you would show forth disease and perhaps death in accordance with the belief-law.

Now, through your understanding of the inner Lord, you find sickness can be caused by nothing, as well as by a so-called belief cause. People have died from fright over mistaken telegrams. When you perceive the fact that you are the Son of the living God, you are not subject to such belief any longer. No sooner is this conquest made than you move to a new mental environment and automatically find that the former law is nil as far as you are concerned, and when the prince of the negative belief comes to you, there is no response.

Do you see why it is you are commanded to take your attention away from the body and away from appearances and place it on the inner Lord—the Christ within—and to be still, and know that *I* am God? When you obey this command, you will find yourself automatically rising to a new and wonderful level of expression in a place where you are not affected by the former things.

Many people fret and worry about expression; they claim they are ready to express but can find no opportunity to do so. You might just as well say that when you throw the ballast from a balloon, the balloon would remain at the same level. It is automatic and takes care of itself. That is why you will cease the everlasting running to and fro, looking for something on the outside, and go within your consciousness and partake of the glorious food of Spirit and drink of the living waters—yea, both figuratively and literally.

A thorough examination will tell you exactly what is the matter. You know better than anyone else—you may not want to face it. Few people like to look upon the Truth; It blinds them, just as it blinded Saul. It is too wonderful and too penetrating and calls for a letting go of many things in order that the realities of the kingdom can be made manifest— within and without. It does not require the sacrifice of a single thing, but by so doing, you are given an infinitely greater manifestation. Glorious—glorious light, dazzling and white, the very light which is to become flesh and dwell among you.

If you are not expressing, you will find that a certain amount of ballast is to be released before you can get to the point of expression. Just as soon as you are willing, the power works and expresses. How? Automatically. When we say "automatically," it carries with it a joyous meaning. You will begin to see that the expression *then* is like the coming of dawn—everything so perfect, so easy, so gloriously successful and so unique, so full of infinite charm.

Beloved, it is so wonderful, this new revelation. "Come apart from them and be ye separate." "Go in and shut the door … and thy Father which seeth in secret will reward you openly." Why do you try to get the reward before you drop out the ballast? You make it hard. Why do you "kick against the pricks"? Why will you doubt? Arise, awake; get thee up. When you are willing and ready, *I* will do the works—and that *I* is within you, your very own point of consciousness where the impersonal life flows through into expression.

"Those whom God hath joined together let no man put asunder." The body and soul become one; the Word becomes flesh; you are not a body separate from your Christ. You are not double-eyed. When you once see, the Word becomes flesh. "Yet in my flesh shall I see God." Do you believe that—right in your flesh? Do you believe that it searches the joints and marrow? Do you see that the two becoming one, instead of having two eyes, have one? Instead of having two opinions, have but one. When the eye is single, the whole body is full of light. When you stop believing in a material man with a Christ-man in the invisible, you will have one—the resurrected and ascended Christ—and you will know that the resurrected Christ had flesh and bones, and ate and drank.

It is wonderful; filled with glorious revelation. When you contemplate this, you immediately feel the overflow of spiritual substance watering your desert (body) and bringing it into freshness and holiness, expression and joy. "My ways are not your ways, saith the Lord." Whose *way* do you want? Your way hasn't amounted to much thus far, has it? Why don't you repent—change?

A new day dawns. Do you hear, you who read? Do you hear the word of your inner Lord? "Behold, I stand at the door and knock: if any man hear my voice, and open the door, I will come in to him and will sup with him and he with me."

Do you know what it means to "break bread with the inner Lord"? It means that the eyes of the blind are opened. When the Christ breaks bread with the disciple, the eyes of the disciple are opened, and he beholds the things which cannot be put into words. He begins to see the revelation of that which is not caught by the human reason and intellect—the deep things of Spirit, which are filled with beauty and holiness and glorious expression; the wonderful invitation to "come and see" —not that "a spirit hath not flesh and bones" but that a Christ-man is a normal, glorious, real manifestation. It is wonderful.

Do you see? Do you begin to understand the saying "He that believeth on me hath everlasting life"? Do you believe that? And just what do you mean by the word *everlasting*? You must begin to answer these things for yourself and seek out the deep, hidden, spiritual substance—the manna that your fathers knew not and of which, "if a man eat, he shall never see death."

"Memory is the only thing which grief can call its own" is the line of an old song. Memory is the only thing that habit can call its own, or evil or revenge or hatred—any of the evils that the human man is subject to. You can see why it is said, "The former things shall not come into mind nor be remembered anymore." With the introduction of the leaven of Christ in the midst of the meal of human understanding, the whole mass begins to change its base, to take on a different quality, and the ballast that is thrown over is memory of evil.

The subconscious mind is the storehouse of memory of every evil thing. It is filled with all the little hates and fears from the very beginning of the human life. You can understand why this will eventually disintegrate and go away because it is the repository of all evil. Without it, man would seek no revenge. Its governing law is "When I would do good, I do evil"—and strange as it may seem, it has been given many of the qualities of the superconscious mind.

We have attributed to this subconscious mind the power to do all sorts of things that it is thoroughly incapable of doing. "He, watching over Israel, neither slumbers nor sleeps" is what awakens you at an appointed hour, and it is this great and glorious superconscious mind that frees you into expression when you are ready to forget yourself. It is this glorious thing that plays and dances, sings and paints, and does everything that is done through millions of avenues of expression. And this is your Christ-Self that stands at the door of your consciousness and knocks for admission. It is too wonderful. "Be still, and know that I am God."

The old idea of getting a mental picture and then praying and begging and beseeching—yea, even demanding—that it appear has given place to the new consciousness that knows that before the human man asks, the superconsciouness has supplied.

We see a case of this kind in the incident of Jesus meeting the disciples at the seaside after the Resurrection. He asked if they had anything to eat, to which they said no. And then Jesus produced the cooked fish and bread for them.

It is wonderful. Before they ask, *I*—the I AM, the Christ-Consciousness—will answer, but it takes pure and unadulterated belief in God to have this take place. It does not take argument or words or listening to theories; it takes pure and unadulterated acceptance of the Truth. A child can have it—what about you? Look to this day; look to your consciousness and see wherein you do err. "Who did hinder you that ye should not obey the truth?" It is wonderful.

Beloved, do you begin to see the glorious possibilities before you? "Come eat, drink without price." Do you hear? Can you obey by throwing over the ballast of human belief and partaking of this holy breaking of the bread of Spirit?

No matter who you are or how prodigal you have been, it is always the same. You, too, can open wide the door and let this Christ into your life—into your very body-temple. You, too, can make the resurrection from the tomb of your dead beliefs and see the glorious, spiritualized flesh of the Son of the living God.

Automatically it will work. "I come as a thief in the night." The appearance of the Christ is neither with noise nor with thinking, for "in a moment when you think not" (when you are not trying to demonstrate Me), then the I AM comes into expression. It is wonderful. Praise God—you are alive and thrilling with the new substance of life, the flesh made Spirit and the Spirit made flesh, the perfect redemption—wholeness. No more the sick body worked upon by an outside force but the body of Spirit—substance, manifesting more and more of the picture shown to you on the Mount of Transfiguration.

It is too wonderful for words—you thrill with the *feel* of the presence of this glorious power. Awake, thou that sleepest. The spiritualized substance of the resurrected Lord is not marked by the passage of time or memory. What was true of man in his former estate is no longer real or effective.

With this consciousness comes the awakening of fresh capacities and talents. You become aware of a new and wonderful power and a sense of relaxation that is the essence of effortlessness, which enables you to give an unlabored performance of the work you have in hand. It is glorious. It is wonderful.

"Then did their hearts burn within them." The manifestation of the burning bush takes place; a flaming fire that destroys nothing that is real. There is found in the final analysis that nothing is left to be destroyed, but everything to be filled with the spirit of the Lord. Then will the blind understand and see, and know that they have always seen. The Man of Spirit, the Christ, has always seen all things. When He is let into conscious expression in the life of man, he searches the joints and marrow; the whole temple of man becomes the glorious temple of the living God, and from that moment onward it is a matter of revelation.

One limitation after another begins to fall away, and new and more glorious precepts come to light. You have just started on the process of self-revelation, and the hidden things that were there always are beginning to come into the light of reality. Be still, be so very still, and cease from "man, whose breath is in his nostrils." Cease from the noisy-talking individual who is always going to tell you a system or a way or means of demonstrating. *I* speak directly. *I* speak of Him that sent me, and *I* speak a varied language. *I* speak with unknown tongues, unknown to those who are still heckling about the letter of Truth. They cannot understand because they have a house divided against itself. They have the Christ and Jesus parted asunder. They have their body separated from their soul, and so they function under the double law which spells disaster.

The human mind is perverse, for the simple reason that it has gone prodigal and formulated all its ideas by judging from appearances. It has seemingly set up many hurdles over which it forces itself to jump, complaining the while that it cannot do so. All this is done in the spirit of human bravado that looks for the "well done" of the relative world.

"Be not afraid, it is I" —but they *were* afraid, and so is the old human self; that is why it keeps on denying the Christ and will not open the door and let Him in. It knows that much rubbish has to go. It knows that the activity of Spirit will cause the sluggishness of procrastination and waiting to disappear. "Be not anxious" —you have but to open the door, by recognizing the Christ within. If you are willing to do this, the rest is automatic. The Christ enters automatically—yea, the Christ, the spiritual substance becoming flesh, enters and searches the joints and marrow, the fibers and nerves and bones of the temple, until the whole house is alive with the life of Christ. It is a glory and a light set upon a hill; it cannot be hid or destroyed. Glory be to God —it is well, and so it is.

You and your risen Lord—alone, and yet for the first time not alone. Wholeness, completeness, content-ment. It is wonderful. The Spirit has become flesh. You are free; the ballast has been thrown overboard, and you automatically ascend to the new level of expression. "My ways" ... "My ways ... " Just saying it within causes an up-gush of Spirit within you. "My ways are not your ways." Aren't you glad?

Chapter Fourteen

The Letter and the Spirit

... singing masons building roofs of gold.

—*Henry V*

The textbooks of today will become the ABC books of tomorrow for all those who have eyes to see. What a world of good came to you out of the little ABC book which you have long since cast aside. What secrets it contained and what mighty doors it opened to you, and yet you have cast it aside.

Yes, you have cast it aside, even as a reference book, though not a day goes by that you do not use the entire substance of the little ABC book. In other words, you took the spirit of the thing and left the letter behind. It was the spirit of it that opened the doors of the universe. By the use of it, you could explore any country and language and understand and read the thoughts of men long since gone from sight. It is a wonderful thing, and yet only valuable when it becomes part and parcel of you.

As long as you are blundering over the letters from one to another, it is not very productive of results, but once you have grasped the understanding and imbibed its spirit, it starts on its magnificent unfoldment and has no end. By it, great avenues of contact are established. And yet, I repeat, the actual book has gone; you care nothing for it; you do not look back upon it with regret. So when the letter of anything goes, the spirit comes. "If I (the personal) go, the Comforter shall come" — that is, the revelation of the Spirit will come.

The one who never lets go of his ABC book is found to be either a fool or an idiot. At least he is considered, in the parlance of the world, as subnormal. "The letter killeth, but the Spirit giveth light." When you begin to see this, you will begin to understand that it is only the spirit of the Truth that will be anything to you, and you will begin to give up the dead formula.

It is "by my spirit, saith the Lord" — "not by might, nor by power." Not by force or effort but by "my spirit." By the Spirit which is hidden in the letter, you shall be able to set free the new expression. The Spirit is like the life of a seed. The shell must first fall away before the plant can be made alive. The shell must first be destroyed before the life can come into manifestation. So is it with the Word. The letter must drop by the way, and the Spirit must be released. It is wonderful and glorious. Heaven and earth are filled with the revelation of Almighty God. Do you hear, you who read this page?

Do you see back of the letter the Spirit shining through—the Spirit which has wrapped up in It the means of complete expression? "All that the Father hath is mine" is true and is correct. But gazing upon the letter and trying to make it so is like expecting tropical flowers to grow in the northern blasts. But cast the letter aside and release the Spirit, and revelation comes to you. It is like magic. Why? Because It has a way of Its own, a means of coming into manifestation that manmade laws cannot even put into words. "No man knoweth the Son, but the Father." It is wonderful.

Why do you not release the letter from your life and see the glorious Spirit work out into expression? The signs will follow. Remember that as soon as the seed is cast into the ground, into the secret place, the shell, or letter, of it starts to drop away and releases the new life and beauty.

Faith as a grain of mustard seed is no good unless the shell of the letter is broken and cast aside and the life of the seed allowed to appear. The glorious promises that you repeat over and over are all filled with the possibility of manifestation. It is the adherence to the letter that killeth—over and over, the same pattern day after day with no results, but with the irritating knowledge that it is all there.

When you stop trying and cast your burden on the I AM and actually are ready to let the Spirit move in and through you, then you will see that the Spirit giveth life and power and that you are suddenly ushered into a new state. Right where you are—right in the place you stand, right in the present surroundings—the transformation takes place because by the power of the Spirit are you made to see that which eternally is and always has been—in other words, the kingdom of heaven here and now. The Spirit of the Word reveals the concrete manifestation. It is then that the Word becomes flesh and dwells among you. Just as you may hold in your hand a dried rosebush and talk for hours to a group of people about a rose. If they had never seen one they would only have the vaguest idea what it looked like, even after you had described it. But cast it into the ground, and then your very words will become flesh and they will see the rose, which in one instant will convey more than a thousand lectures could.

Do you see? It takes the faith of a child, for the adult cannot let go and would rather talk about "how and why" and "when and where" and would rather spend hours pointing out what is wrong with other members of the universe than spend one moment trying to rid his own sight of the beam that is out-picturing everything evil.

If I wear a pair of dark goggles, the whole world, so far as I am concerned, is gray or dark, but that does not make it so. If you look through eyes of limitation and ugliness, everything appears so to you. Even God becomes a God of wrath, and Jesus becomes a hard taskmaster, regardless of the regaling statement and promise, "I came that your joy might be full" and "I came not to destroy, but to fulfill."

Do you see? The Power is here, not to destroy but to fulfill the Law, to fulfill the glorious promises.

All these little points of evil that seem to be giving you so much trouble will be picked up into the positive expression of Good — *here* and *now*. It is wonderful and it is glorious. God is everywhere, and beside Him there is naught else.

"Let not your heart be troubled: ye believe in God, believe also in me." Where is the *Me*? "Believe, and ye shall be saved." Do you see the power of the word *believe*? It is pure *acceptance* of the Word in the face of the most adverse testimony. When the appearances are as far removed as the rosebush is from the rose, the "belief" — acceptance — will cause the holy promise to be released.

Do you see why "Then went he in and shut the door" has its importance to you as never before? Argument and talk about these precious things will only bring the ugly futility of the letter. The letter without the Spirit is *dead*. Do you hear? It is dead, of no use.

The books that we are reading today on Truth will be the ABC books of tomorrow; we will have imbibed the spirit of them and dropped the letter aside. Why? Because the textbooks of the future will have to do with things that we only casually mention at this time. From time to time, we hear of levitation, of fourth-dimensional expression, of the Superman, and of many things that could not be told us back in Jerusalem. These will form the basis of the textbooks of the future, for the spirit of the present teaching will be released to such an extent that sickness, sin, and unhappiness will be unknown: it will be so generally understood that no one will stop to marvel at the working of the law of the Absolute.

There was a time when a man who knew how to read was outstanding in a community, but today it would be an exception to come upon one who could not. So is it with the Word. Just so soon as you release the Spirit from the letter, the things that take place from the standpoint of Spirit are bound to appear. "Glory to God in the highest, peace on earth, goodwill toward men."

"Be still ... I have many things to say to you." When we learn to be still and not talk constantly to the Divine, we are beginning to experience the deep, hidden things of the Spirit. New doors are opened to us, new avenues of expression, and the unafraid state of consciousness becomes manifest to us.

"The former things shall pass away; they shall not be remembered nor come into mind anymore." The shell that releases the living plant shall be forgotten. It shall not be remembered nor come into mind any more. You could not put the flower back into the seed, nor can you put man back into the limitations of a state of consciousness from which he has freed himself. When you are freed from a certain state of consciousness, you are not subject to any of the laws which formerly operated therein—just as the flower which has released itself from the seed is not under any of the laws that applied to the seed.

For example, a bird or animal might have carried the seed away, or it might have been left upon the shelf and destroyed by insects. As the flower comes under the care of the gardener, it has protection and a new set of laws and environment.

This illustration, as all illustrations, is inadequate to convey the idea of the wonderful change that goes on when the "shell" of the letter is cracked and the new idea—the Spirit—is released. "The Lord, he it is that doth go before thee; he will be with thee; he will not fail thee." Fear not—when you cast your burden on the Lord, He will sustain thee.

For eye hath not seen, nor ear heard, neither have entered into the heart of man ... (1Cor. 2:9).

Be still ... be still ... be still and listen for the revelation to be made. Close the material eyes that are hypnotized by the serpent of appearances and see the revelation that is coming into manifestation, "casting all your care upon him; for he careth for you."

"He that abideth in me, and I in him, the same bringeth forth much fruit." If you abide in this consciousness—this *believing* consciousness—then you shall bring forth much manifestation. It is the following of a natural law, a law which is stated in terms of grace—divine intervention, divine influence. All knees shall bend at the name (nature) of Christ. Every temporal power shall come tumbling to the ground. Every golden calf shall be brought low, and the kingdom shall be established *here* and *now*.

The New Dimension of life enters only from a point within and never from without. The oak tree proceeds from the Center, which is in reality only a point where the already finished thing makes itself visible. Through our limited thought it seems to grow, but when we can "look again," we will see "the flower before the seed." What we see as growth is *reality* appearing. "Before you ask" tells this revelation. It is.

Chapter Fifteen

Abundance

He which soweth sparingly shall reap sparingly; and he which soweth bountifully shall reap bountifully. Every man according as he purposeth in his heart, so let him give; not grudgingly or of necessity: for God loveth a cheerful giver.

—2 Cor. 9:7

The sowing lavishly and abundantly comes from the knowledge of Infinite Substance. The sowing for increase in order that the storehouses may be filled and the soul may take its ease always results in death to the idea. The abandon of abundant sowing shows absolute faith in the Unseen.

We are beginning to see that the law of substance is diametrically reversed from that which is usually accepted. We are first called upon to give abundantly—give out of our lack as it were, but give lavishly. The widow's mite was more than most gifts because it was given abundantly; it was given freely and from the heart. The motive ye mete "shall be measured to you again," and "it shall be pressed down, shaken together and running over." The motive back of the abundant sowing will determine the harvest. If the sowing is done with gain as the one idea in mind, then the looked-for results are not forthcoming.

"There is he that scattereth, yet tendeth to increase, and there is he that withholdeth and tendeth towards poverty." We see that the symbol is a poor thing to hold on to. The more you have your attention fixed on the symbol, the less opportunity you have of grasping the reality back of it.

All this indication of abandoned and abundant sowing is the result of fearlessness on the part of the sower. He that does not follow the command "Launch out into deep waters" cannot have the big fish. He will never find them near the shore, just as a person will never learn to swim as long as he keeps one foot on the ground and stays in shallow water. "Launch out into deep waters." Do, dare, and be silent. Dare to enlarge the borders of your tent. Dare to sow abundantly and without abandon, and rest in the perfect knowledge that the bread which you have thus broken has been broken to increase. You will learn presently that only what you give you get. A seed given to the universe gives back its usefulness and increase. An idea given to the universe gives forth its joy, and its increase comes home to the giver. "The signs follow; they do not precede."

Joyously abandon yourself to the Christ within and care not for the increase. It must come of its own volition. "Be careful about nothing" is the command to the understanding heart. This being careful about nothing means also to be careless about nothing. The command to be careful about nothing can only be used by one who has begun to see the superabundance of everything in the universe. The substance of God is everywhere present. Yet all this joyous abandon does not imply license; it implies liberty — liberty of the Sons of God, which, when once tasted and experienced, brings to the consciousness of man the true concept of freedom. The command goes forth, "Be not again entangled." Go not back to the former bondage, the sowing sparingly. Sow abundantly and reap abundantly — with the glorious abandon of the Sons of the living God.

On the same day Jesus saw a man working on the Sabbath-day, he said to him: "Man, if thou knowest what thou doest, thou art blessed; but if thou knowest not, thou art cursed, and a transgressor of the law" (Cambridge MS. Codex Bezae).

He that sows abundantly, thinking thereby to gain a thousandfold that which he sows, knows not what he does and is cursed, insomuch as he loses all. Trying to use God as a stock exchange whereby you can gain personal ends is to entirely defeat the principle of Truth so far as you are concerned. We learn to sow abundantly because we are seeing the abundant blessings that are poured into our life, and we are coming to the point of unafraidness. We are more and more coming to the place of recognition of the presence of God as being literally the sufficiency of all things.

Man is slowly evolving from what might be called the degree of the egg. As an egg, he is perfectly helpless, though he may contain all knowledge of the power of God. He has no power of self-locomotion. Were an egg in the path of an oncoming car, no matter how much it knew its protection, it could not escape the dire effects of meeting with destruction. When the chick is hatched, it may yet rest in the same place, but it has power to sidestep the oncoming danger. So man, when he first learns of the Truth, finds out many things that he knows to be absolutely true while he is in the egg degree, yet he can only put them into practice in a very limited degree because of the shell of personality that is around him.

But presently he throws off the shell and comes to the degree higher, where he is able to avoid much of the so-called evil. He can step aside, as it were, and he is able to prove the parables and promises of the Bible instead of knowing inwardly that they are true but not being able to see them into manifestation.

"Man, if thou knowest what thou doest ..." If you know what you are doing as the Son of the living God, you shall cause the dry seed of parable and promise to crack open and give forth its substance. You will know what it means to "be careful about nothing."

All things are possible to the awakened soul. As is recorded in Acts 2, the speaking with new tongues took place before an infinite number of men of different races and languages, yet all understood. Twenty different tongues understood one single voice, although they could not understand each other. This fourth-dimensional picture of the concrete use of the Law gives us a glimpse of how the impossible becomes possible, and how every human law is reversed and found to be productive of results. You will begin to see that it is useless to argue about the real Truth underlying these great statements, for the Truth is so intangible and impossible to reason out —it completely escapes the wisdom of man.

> Be strong and of a good courage, fear not, nor be afraid of them: for the Lord thy God, he it is that doth go with thee: he will not fail thee, nor forsake thee (Deut. 31:6).

Can you, you who read this promise, accept it literally? Can you accept the fact that the Lord thy God goes with you and that He is the One that makes twenty nations understand a single tongue, though they cannot understand each other? Do you believe this? "I will walk in them and talk in them" —why need you worry further about the safety of your goings and comings? And why worry about the word you will carry into the universe? The word that comes from the speaking of the inner Lord is the word that shall not return to you void "but shall accomplish whereunto it is sent."

Beloved! Are you beginning to see the glorious sense of abandon and rest that is due to come into manifestation in your life the moment you take the promises of the Lord and tear off the hard shell of human reasoning that you have put around them? Rejoice, and be exceeding glad, "for it is your Father's good pleasure to give you the kingdom of heaven." A gift must be accepted. Through the rejoicing, there is recognition of the infinite Abundance that is manifested in ways that no man can find out, just as the message is given by one person to twenty different races—one speaking, twenty hearers all hearing differently, yet all understanding the Voice. Awake, thou that sleepest. A new day is dawning, and when I say *a new day is dawning*, I do not mean the symbolic day of former years, but a wonderful New Day of expression and abundance wherein you will experience the glorious revelation that the Lord is walking *in* you and talking *in* you.

Look up, then, and rejoice, for "Thou meetest him that rejoiceth and worketh righteousness, those that remember thee in thy ways."

Rejoice and be glad. The ground you stand upon is holy ground, and you are clad in the garments of Light and Praise. A new day dawns and a new door opens before you. It is well. Rejoice and scatter abundantly the glorious idea of Truth. Live abundantly the Life in the inexhaustible source of *all* Life. Verily, if you will prove the Law with the fearless faith of one who permits the Voice to speak through him and the Power to walk in him, you shall see that the windows of heaven are opened to you, and the blessings that are poured out are too many for you to receive, so small has been your human concept of the abundance of God.

You are learning the glorious relaxation of the prodigal who has returned to his Father's house and is finding again the wonderful Truth:

> For I am persuaded, that neither death, nor life, nor angels, nor principalities, nor powers, nor things present, nor things to come, nor height, nor depth, nor any other creature, shall be able to separate us from the love of God, which is in Christ Jesus our Lord (Rom. 8:39).

Chapter Sixteen

The Other Disciple

Then went in also that other disciple ...
—John 20:8

The other disciple who went into the tomb and found it empty is, symbolically speaking, you. It is you who have experienced all the manifestations of the Christ-Consciousness — the healing of sickness and sin, the transformation of one substance into another, the supplying of all things needful, and the overcoming of gravitation, yes, the raising from the dead — and now you have come to a place where proof is given you of self-resurrection. The swaddling clothes (bondage) of the babe become the graveclothes eventually left in the tomb. They are the human bondages that must sooner or later be laid aside for the robes that are white and glistening, the garments of Light and Praise.

Eventually you are brought face to face with the fact that in the final analysis self-resurrection will take place. "I have power to pick it up or lay it down." Until a man comes to the place of the "other disciple" and goes *in*, he will be toying still with the idea that his help comes from some other source than God. It is true that up to a certain point much help is given, but after a while the disciple is left to himself. He must either perform the process of self-resurrection, which is put in various terminology, or go the way of all flesh. He must be born again, and this "borning" must be from within. It is manifested within each person; it is a personal and individual experience that no one else can do for you.

"Marvel not" — do not be surprised when these things come to you; your eyes will not always be "holden that thou shall not know him." You will not always walk to Emmaus with the Master and fail to see him. The scales will drop from your eyes, and you will perceive the things which eyes have not seen and ears have not heard and the things that you have not yet thought of.

It takes more than the human sense to recognize when anything has truly happened. The human sense did not recognize Jesus when he presented his risen body. Why? Because the human sense first judges from the intellectual standpoint, which says emphatically that no one when dead rises again. If they rise, they were not really dead, or else a miracle happened.

Go thou in and shut the door, and contemplate the Presence—then you will see the nothingness of all the evils to which the flesh is heir.

"These things have I spoken unto you in proverbs: but the time cometh, when I shall no more speak unto you in proverbs, but I shall show you plainly." Surely there is no ambiguity about this statement, "I shall show you plainly." The one who is ready, who has passed beyond the curious stage and who is not looking for signs and wonders, who is not searching for the loaves and the fishes, will see. He will hear the things which could not be told because formerly he could not bear to hear them. "When the student is ready, the Master appears." "Be still, and know that I am God" is more than a statement. It is not something to be talked about—it is something to experience. "Then went in that other disciple." You are standing on the threshold of the glorious experience of self-resurrection. You are at the point of receiving the revelation.

> Hitherto have ye asked for nothing in my name; ask and ye shall receive, that your joy may be full (John 16:24).

How can your joy be anything else but full when you begin to see—through the thick under-growth of human reasoning—the Garden of Eden to which you are returning? It is enough to make you thrill with joy, for all the fond imaginations that have strayed over your soul without expression are now understood. The single ear, the single eye, the single voice—you have come away from the tower of Babel, that great galaxy of people who are all shouting in their own tongue that they have the only way to reach heaven and that you must follow them or be lost; who have finally succeeded in building up nothing but a tower of jealousy, strife, and hatred. All talking different tongues—confusion. Come away from it all. Seek the inner Lord and listen to the glorious revelation that is made to you now.

And as we have borne the image of the earthly, we shall also bear the image of the heavenly (1 Cor. 15:49).

When the self-resurrection takes place, you shall transform the fleshly body to one of Spirit. The Lord shall become flesh and dwell among you. The body shall take on new properties, and you shall then be no more under the laws of the dense matter that has caused you so much grief. "If ye be in the Spirit, ye are no more under the law." You are then under grace—glorious freedom and cancellation from the mistaken evils of the flesh.

Why not, since you functioned under the law "When I would do good, I do evil?" Who could blame you for doing evil if you did it in spite of the fact that you wanted to do good? Not any just God. You are beginning to understand why it is that repentance makes a full cancellation for the evil that functioned in your life, and how you are under grace when you are in the Spirit. The "other disciple" who goes *in* experiences the new birth, and to him are revealed the hidden mysteries.

"The first man is of the earth, earthy; the second man is the Lord from heaven." Where is heaven? According to Jesus, it is a state of consciousness. It is within you, and descending out of this heavenly consciousness will come the Lord—the risen Lord.

As the shell of a seed gives way, life appears. As the muddy vesture of human thought that has enclosed you falls away, the Christ comes into manifestation; is unwrapped from his graveclothes and set free. Do not be disheartened; it is stated in the Law that "it is sown in a natural body; it is raised a spiritual body." When you are willing to let go of the human beliefs that you have massed together by judging from appearances, then you will raise the spiritual body. That is, you will see the Spirit become flesh and dwell among you. It is wonderful.

> Flesh and blood cannot inherit the kingdom of God (1 Cor. 15:50).

We understand that the laws of the flesh, which are constantly changing and bringing inharmony to the individual, cannot inherit the kingdom. The flesh-and-blood man has not the capacity to accept so much good. He has functioned in such uncertain capacities that he hardly knows what is right and what is wrong.

"Why seek ye the living among the dead?" Why look for that which is living in the midst of that which is dead? Why do you seek in the dead letter for the Spirit, which in reality dwells eternally within you?

"Then went that other disciple in." Be still—"I shall come as a thief in the night."

You are the other disciple. Why don't you go "in" and discover your permanent Identity, and begin *now* to live in the kingdom?

Chapter Seventeen

The Mighty Atom

We are already touching, though as it were only with our fingertips, a new source of power so great as to make us inexhaustibly wealthy.

An atom is defined as an invisible particle of matter so minute that it cannot be divided. The very definition of it goes beyond the ken of human reason since it is impossible for the human mind to think of a particle of matter so small that it could not be divided; hence, at the very start, we are faced with a pure mental proposition. Yet scientists tell us that the atom is made up of an infinite number of electrons, which are further described as centers of force.

> We all know that the atoms of which everything is made up are themselves made up of a "cloud of electrons," at the center of which is a tiny heart or nucleus made up of the tightest jam known of the smallest electric particles known (*Sunday Express*, London, January 19, 1932).

In spite of the definition of an atom as being indivisible, we now discover that it has been split and thereby changed in nature. This is almost beyond the imagination of the average person, and yet it seems to hark back to the abstract idea of "faith as a grain of mustard seed" being able to move mountains and do all sorts of things that are impossible to the human sense.

The article from which the above quotation was taken is by Gerald Heard, and he continues to say:

> If you could knock out some of these particles, you would then change the nature of the atom; you would have made the dream of the alchemists come true; you would be able to transmute elements, you would be able to change, if not lead, then quite possibly mercury, into gold.

What Mr. Heard promises by "knocking out some of these particles" seems to be in perfect alignment with the power as used by Jesus in changing one substance into another and changing the nature and quantity of the manifestation. Jesus changed water into wine. He saw beyond the limitations of the human mind and was able to release the infinite substance into expression in whatsoever form was needed.

Every knee shall bend to the Christ, and we shall finally see that He is King, and that His wisdom makes the wisdom of the world as naught. One premise after another is reached in physics and discarded, but the laws of the Master remain intact and changeless; little by little, we find it useless to try to bring them down to our level of thinking and reasoning.

The Mighty Atom which is within you is the Christ-Consciousness which has been bound by the human belief. When the shell of human limitations is broken, the Mighty Atom of your true Self comes into expression and sets aside all the laws of the human mind, no matter how time-honored they may be.

We read things in the daily papers that would have caused people to be burned as witches not so long ago. Man is getting back to pure abstractions, into the invisible—and finding it more real than the visible. Mr. Heard says, "Common sense—and this is becoming commoner and commoner as science advances—has again let us down." Man is beginning to see that the Master stated it clearly when he said, "The wisdom of man is foolishness in the eyes of God."

Professor Jeans declares there is no such thing as ether, and if this be true (and he seems satisfied that he has proven it to be so), then another cherished basis for calculation of the present universe has gone from under us.

"I shall overturn and overturn until he comes whose place it is to rule." The handwriting on the wall is that not one stone of human reason shall be left upon another and that he—the pure, unadulterated wisdom of God—shall come to reign in peace. That is, the reign of harmony and order shall be made manifest despite the chaos of human thinking.

We have kept on saying, "Common sense shows that the world must have this or that, and so this or that must be there." But when we look, we find that the things said to be necessary by common sense have not in fact been found necessary in making this surprising world.

The recognition of this Mighty Atom at the center of your being is what causes you to take the first step in releasing it into expression. "Behold, I stand at the door and knock" — the heart of the Atom is alive and knocking against the shell of human belief, knocking to come out into expression in your life and to bring with it the glorious power which will transcend the human limitations.

The Cosmic Ray

By giving up the ether, we are taking another and a big step out of the common, dull world we have imagined to be real, into the real world where perhaps anything is possible.

But though, through this discovery, space has been found to be emptier than we thought possible, through another find it has been discovered to be far fuller than we suspected. Scientists are continuing to measure the cosmic radiation.

This radiation is called cosmic because it comes not from any star but from out the blackness of space where we thought there was absolutely nothing — save the ether which has failed to materialize.

The existence of this radiation was never suspected till quite lately, yet it is at present the most powerful thing known in the universe. It can penetrate sixteen feet of lead, when X-rays are easily stopped by less than an inch.

And now Sir James Jeans has just suggested that, though it is only today that we have been able to pick it up, it is a radiation which was sent out at the beginning of the universe

—G. Heard, *Sunday Express*
London, January 10, 1932

Already the radiation of the Star which is leading back to the Christ-Consciousness is being felt by the scientist. Where is the light of this Cosmic Ray leading but back to the very center of Power? Just as the wise men and shepherds symbolically followed its light to the manger, so today the scientist and the metaphysician are following this light on to powers which are only dreamed of at this time, of which Christ not only spoke but demonstrated and said were the heritage of every man. It is through the door of acceptance and recognition of the existence of such a power that men are willing to push forward, following the emanation of this ray which all the time is getting brighter and more iridescent; more manifold in its manifestation.

"I have a way that ye know not of." Within you lies this Mighty Atom of power and strength — within you lies the possibility of bringing out this glorious expression. There is a reason for the hope that is in us. We are following the light of the Star, back to the very Babe that is born unto us and upon whose shoulders shall be the government.

Come apart from among them and be ye separate (2 Cor. 6:17).

The principle of everything we see in the universe today, no matter how wonderful it may be, has existed always, just as the principle back of the splitting of the atom, and the further revelations that will ensue, are here today and just as usable as they will be when man discovers them. "You have not chosen me—I have chosen you." The Power has chosen you to be the glorious expression, and the only way this expression can take place is for the Mighty Atom of your being to be set free, for the Christ to come into expression by being recognized.

The great Cosmic Ray which is beyond the stars seems to point at something that is the All-powerful, emanating from the throne of God. It is well.

And now men talk of a "cosmic glue" with which the particles of the *heart* of the "indivisible" atom are held together. And again the question, "Who can know the mind of God?" Is the "unified field theory" yet complete?

Chapter Eighteen

"For God So Loved the World"

When you are ready—
I will do the works through you.

"For God so loved the world, that he gave his only begotten Son, that whosoever believeth in him should not perish, but have everlasting life" (John 3:16).

Suddenly, like a burst of light that pierces the dark clouds of night, comes the revelation that God so *loved* the world—yes, this very world that you have been calling hell; that you have found so full of everything evil; that you have been trying to die out of or trying to escape. Yes, this very world God has *loved*.

It must be that we have hypnotized ourselves into something that is unlovely. Yet we find that God so *loved* the world. If God had found it one-tenth as evil as we have been taught to believe it is, He would certainly not have loved it; He would have destroyed it. Can it be that we, you and I, are mistaken regarding the world—have we been seeing through a glass, darkly, and mistaking the shadows of the human belief for the reality, to such an extent that we have come to hate that which God loved?

"Awake, thou that sleepest, and Christ shall give thee Light" — the Light which will enable you to start the Love process and set yourself free from the prison house of your own making.

"When *you* are ready ... "

"If you cannot love those whom you see, how can you love God whom you do not see?" A question asked and passed over too lightly. The same thing might be asked, "If you cannot love the world which you can see, how can you love the kingdom which you cannot see?" It is time that we awakened from the mesmeric sleep that we have cast over ourselves. We have been stupefied by the heavy drug called procrastination. Half the people who are "knowing the truth" are merely waiting for something in the future to happen and are at the same time despising the present manifestation.

There be those who will say, "Love not the world," and by the word *world*, they mean just the antithesis of what is meant when it is stated that "God so loved the world." It is made quite clear that if we cannot love our fellow creatures, we cannot love God. And eventually we begin to see that we glorify that which we love. The power of love that is within every man is the power to transform appearances. "Love never faileth" would indicate that all else can fail. Also, "Perfect love casteth out fear." We are beginning to see the power of Love. When we love our fellow beings, they become Godlike and display Godlike qualities. And when we love the earth as God loved it, then we transform it into heaven.

Self-examination shows, however, that to most of us this world is just a battleground. Each morning we rise and set forth to battle evil, always looking for ways and means of overcoming the almost insurmountable obstacles that arise before us like a Goliath. This fighting spirit stays with us, in spite of the command, "Ye do not need to fight—set yourselves, and see the salvation of the Lord."

In the beautiful God-loved world, there is nothing to fight, but in the world of man's creating, he finds evil everywhere. It is for man to choose in which of these habitats he will live. Surely, as soon as he sees God in man, man becomes Godlike, and just so surely as he sees heaven here and now, the world becomes again the Garden of Eden—the very garden that God loved. And for this purpose He gave His Son—the Christ—and said that whosoever believed in Him should have everlasting life. The Son is given to each of us when we are ready to accept the priceless gift within ourselves.

"I came not to destroy, but to fulfill." That is the message of the I Am coming into expression in your life. *I* the Christ, the You of You, came not to destroy but to fulfill the law of God and to fulfill and bring out the reason why "God so loved the world." We are missing it all as long as we keep on the hunt after evil. We are missing the great and grand issue of life when we keep pounding away at imaginary beliefs and thinking that our business in the world is to fight evil. "Put up your sword." When you are ready …

> God so loved the world that he gave his only begotten Son, that whosoever believeth in him should not perish, but have everlasting life" (John 3:16).

The idea of a perishing body or kingdom, then, is lost in the consciousness of the everlasting life. Do you think for a moment you can continue everlastingly in the same personality? Do you see this would be quite as impossible as it would be for you to continue a baby forever? The constant revelation that is coming with this imperishable Life is such that it drops off one belief after another and lets the perfect manifestation come into being.

Revelations, one after another, break over the universe of the newly found soul. The former things are remembered no more; they cannot come into mind, for the mind has been made new, and it naturally has nothing in it that answers to the former limitations and beliefs. "The prince of this world (the ugly, hated world that you have been living in) cometh," and findeth nothing in you because you have renewed your mind, and there is nothing in this new state that responds to the former evils and limitations. Do you begin to see the *new* day that is dawning?

Small wonder, then, that the command came, "Go forth, heal the sick, open the prisons," and so forth. How can this be done except the power—the power of revelation—is given with the command? "Where the Spirit of the Lord is, there is liberty." The Spirit is everywhere, and when It is recognized in that place, the limitations of the human belief are suddenly burst asunder and the manifestation is set free.

A shell does not hold a chick one moment after it has grown to the limitations of the shell. When you recognize the presence of God, the limitations that bound you are broken asunder by the sudden expansion of this new knowledge. Be still … do not talk … it is well with thee. *I* am "he that should come"—and you will begin to understand the difference between overcoming and realization, or revelation.

Be still … be still … be still. Remember in your quiet that God *so loved* this world that you are finding so hateful and ugly. Be still … you will see and understand.

The presence of the very God that loved this world is in everything and through everything—even in your hell, in your prison, in your problem—and contains everything for the complete satisfaction of every human desire interpreted in its truest form. Be still … be still. It is well. Right in the midst of it all, there am *I*; and *I* am everything that you can possibly ask or think.

For God *so loved* the world — what are you doing with it? Why did God so love the place that you hate and find so filled with all undesirable things? Be still ... be still ... and see if the Son which was given does not come to abide with you and make all the desires of your heart possible by the process of revelation.

And *God so loved* the world — *loved the world.*
Are you ready? Answer Me — I AM.

Chapter Nineteen

Thou Art the Bright Messenger

Thou art the Bright Messenger—the Shining One, the being of pure Spirit. Thou art not the man thou hast been, lo! these many years.

Thou art newborn, fresh, clean, and pure. Thou art not an old creature patched up by various treatments. Thou, Bright Messenger, Golden One, hast never descended to the level of belief and therefore hast not consorted with the shadows of the play-life.

Thou art the Bright Messenger, with winged feet, who goeth where he will and knoweth no obstruction or condition. Thou art the unconditioned, the untrammeled, the free—the individualized yet inseparable manifestation of the All-God.

Thou art the Bright Messenger. Thou art full of light—bathed in All-Light. Whithersoever thou goest is light—not consciously projected but unconsciously conveyed; a natural effect of thy presence.

Thou art the Bright Messenger. Thine eye is single to the Allness of God, the Oneness of creation. Thou therefore seest with the eye of light. Thou lookest into a universe of All-Light, and seest through the shadows of belief. Thou seest the world in a world, the rose in a rose, and the Man in a man. Thou perceivest with thine eye of Light that which *is* and always has been—not that which shall be changed by begging, beseeching, or praying to a tyrant called God to make whole. With the eye of Light, thou seest nothing to heal, for thy sight is perfect in the understanding.

> I am of too pure eyes to
> behold iniquity (see Hab. 1:13).

If God cannot perceive it, how can the man in the street perceive it and make long prayers over it?

Thou art the Bright Messenger—the being of Light. In the touch of thy hand is light. As the warmth of spring touches the frozen earth, so thy touch of light causes the seed to swell and burst and the flower to leap from her chalice. Thy touch of light is like the soft rain on the parched desert, which causes it to bloom as a rose. Whomsoever thou touchest—in the true sense of the word—thou transformest, instantly, gloriously, freely, joyously. And men shall call it health, but thou shalt call it revelation.

Thou art the Bright Messenger. Thou hast the golden touch which transforms everything into the gold of which Ophir never dreamed. Thy touch shall be able to take from the fish's mouth the needed symbol. Thy touch it is which gives that which is beyond price and which makes a man rich, even when the saying goes "Silver and gold have I none, but of such as I have I give unto thee." Such as thou hast in the touch, O Bright Messenger, is beyond the price of pearls and rubies—the transforming touch which is gentle yet firm, which is soft like the surface of the ocean but which has the power to dash a whole fleet of evil ships into oblivion. Thou art the Bright Messenger—thy touch is golden.

Thou art the Bright Messenger. The aroma of thy presence precedes thee. Thy passing is as the passing of a cloud of incense from the sacred lilies of the enchanted woods. In thy presence, the precious perfume of the soul is sensed above the stagnant odors of human beliefs. When thou comest to the soul, it is as the bridegroom before whom the lovely flowers of purity open and shed their perfume in superabundance. At thy coming, the rose loosens the silken tassel of her soul and gives forth the glorious attar of her being. At thy coming the trees and minerals loosen the glorious, refreshing odors of woods and stones.

From thy nostrils comes the Breath of Life. From thy breath comes the appearance of the new creation. Man becomes a living soul by breathing thy breath—man lives and moves and breathes and has his being in thy breath. Thy breath fans the small sparks of faith into the flame of realization. From thy nostrils comes the flashing, dazzling fire which consumes the dross of belief. Thou art the Bright Messenger.

Thou art the Bright Messenger. Thy invitation is "Oh, taste and see that the lord is good." Eat my body (my substance) and drink my blood (inspiration).

Thy taste is golden. The milk and honey of the universe of the All-God are thine. The hidden manna (that which the eye, the human belief, cannot see) thou feedest upon.

Thy eternal drink is the Living Water. Thou shalt never be without the sustenance of Spirit, no matter whither thou goest. Thou shalt realize this all-substance, and thou shalt cease from thy thought-taking process of wondering wherewithal shall we be clothed and fed. Thou shalt eat, and hunger no more; drink, and thirst no more—for thou shalt feed upon the reality of life instead of the husks of material belief, with its shadow appearances.

Thou art the Bright Messenger, the bearer of glad tidings. Upon thy breastplate, encrusted in gold, is the motto "Speak no evil nor listen to it." Thou art of too pure ears to hear evil—thou hearest with the ear of Spirit. Thou hearest with the silent ear, closed to the din of the human, relative conditions but open to that which "eye hath not seen, ear hath not heard, neither hath it entered into the heart of man (human thought) the things which are prepared for them that love thy Law."

Thou hearest the word of peace, and a whole ocean of fury of belief ceaseth—stilled and made calm. Thou hearest the reports of that which *is*, and thou tellest of these. Thou hearest the things that "ear hath not heard"—the ear of man whose breath is in his nostrils and whose eye is double—and yet thou hearest the report of the kingdom *here* and *now;*

thou hearest the glad tidings of the eternal Christ walking today in the Garden of Attainment. Thou hearest the words, "This is my beloved Son, in whom I am well pleased," and thou recognizest these words as addressed to thee.

Thou art neither ashamed nor afraid because of thy nakedness; the stark tragedies of the human belief fade into the distance when thou answerest this call with the "Aye, Aye" of Spirit. Thou hearest in the truest sense of the word—in the fearless sense of the word—"Arise and shine, for thy light hath come." No need to create this light, to stimulate it, but only to recognize this light as within.

How can a man who is constantly looking for evil to heal and treat know anything of the kingdom? How can he understand the things which cannot be seen or heard with the human ears? How can he set right that which he has already done? And yet there are those poor deluded souls who have appointed themselves the official stone casters for the Christ, not realizing that they are casting stones at Him.

Thou art the Bright Messenger—the Being of Light—the Unafraid. Why should there be fear when the realization has come that thou art the Bright Messenger, the being of pure Spirit—not subject to the beliefs of the thought-world; not subject to the failures and successes of thy human life but suddenly up and above that which has always seemed so real.

Bright Messenger, Unafraid Being, Holy Creature, Son of God—arise, shine. Arise, let thy light so shine. Take no thought; if thou take thought, it will be of fear or limitation. Thou art the Bright Messenger—the Being of Light that goeth forth before the manifestation of thy human self and maketh straight the way. Thou art the Unafraid, the Unbound, the Prometheus Unbound. Thou shalt smite the rock and make it gush forth the living water of Life.

Thou art the Bright Messenger, the Being of Light, the Unafraid. Thou art glorious. Thou art free—thou art not bound by human limitations. "Thou art not another (a separate one) but the same one." Thou art the Christ.

Hail! Soul of Me, I salute you—
Son of God, Christ, Bright Messenger.

Chapter Twenty

Trailing Clouds of Glory

Our birth is but a sleep and a forgetting:
The Soul that rises with us, our life's Star,
Hath had elsewhere its setting,
And cometh from afar:
Not in entire forgetfulness,
And not in utter nakedness,
But trailing clouds of glory do we come
From God, who is our home:
Heaven lies about us in our infancy!
                              —*Wordsworth*

Trailing clouds of glory, sweeping the great horizon of your new heaven and earth, follow after you, Son of the living God, in great swirls of light and illumination. No more can you withhold this wondrous light than day can stay its coming. No more the conscious effort to know the truth; to make others see the truth. No more straining to have people listen to your chatter about what is or is not—no more anything, but simply *being*.

Why do you *try* to be? A thousand eager souls have gone down in defeat trying through every possible means to be that which they already were. "They have taken my Lord away" is the cry of a personality worshipper—one who looks to mankind for his salvation instead of looking to the only possible source of such power—that within his own consciousness.

Trailing clouds of glory follow after you, and the great illumination of their brightness goes before you. Are you afraid to accept such a glorious picture of your true Self? Then you are yet playing with the colored pebbles in the shallow waters of metaphysics—disobeying the command, "Launch out into deep waters." He who has the courage to "launch out" into the freedom of his soul, not asking of those beachcombers who hang around the shores of personal ideas, will find nothing wanting. The rough sea will be smooth, and the calmness shall be there—that deep stillness of being alone and for the first time being actually free from the soul hunger and loneliness that nothing of the human mind can satisfy.

Many who read these lines—perhaps you who are reading now—will be self-revealed and will find it natural for the Son of the living God to have glorious, trailing clouds of attainment follow after him, no matter whither he may go. The signs shall follow—they shall not precede. Why look ye for a signpost, when *I* am the way? Salute no man that thou passest along life's highway, for he may turn you awry. Salute the Soul of your true Self and be not turned aside. "It is I"—eternally *I*—and when you begin to see Me in everything, you will call Me out into expression, and that which flies at you in mad fury trying to destroy you shall be in an instant transformed into Me.

This whole process lies within the scope of you who read this page. I have said to you, "Agree with thine adversary quickly," and the agreement is made through calling the name of the living God out of the dead Lazarus. It is wonderful. Everything is wonderful; the only thing that is dispelled at such a moment is your belief in evil. Even hell is made into heaven when you call upon Me. Call upon Me, and *I* will answer. Do you hear? I said, "*I* will answer."

Believest thou this? Or are you going to argue a little and try to prove that it is so with a reservation? Go thy way; the bridegroom passeth, and you have no oil because you have not learned yet to accept your good. You are still with those who want to make it happen and who are looking for personal aggrandizement.

But one day—perhaps today, perhaps right now—you will shed the filthy rags of argument and of personal teaching, rise and go up into a high place and descend again; not to work out problems but to reveal the God within you. As much as ye will, that give *I* unto you. Do you hear?

"Acquaint now (right while you are reading it now) thyself with him, and be at peace; thereby all good shall come unto you." How very simple, too simple perhaps, because you have been hypnotized into believing that long, hard study was necessary to attain the kingdom, and that you were full of sin that some sin cleanser had to take out of you by special instruction that he could give you. Yet shall I call again and again to you: "Acquaint now thyself with him, and be at peace: thereby all good shall come unto you." Do you see how utterly impossible it would be for you to explain the glorious feeling of "It is well" to anyone who was trying to think it out?

You are impressed with that which descends to the plane of human thinking from the place of Christ-Consciousness, the fourth-dimensional realm. Do you not see what is meant by "Acquaint now thyself with him and be (find yourself) at peace; thereby all (the whole) good shall come unto you." Can you understand, then, that your expression of healing, of whatever belief comes before you, is merely the light of the trailing clouds of glory which automatically emanate from your being?

When you see this, that all (the whole) good shall come unto you, then will you know that you have the hidden well of living water and the exhaustless substance of the manna that cometh down from heaven. Do you see that you will be self-sufficient and that your giving will in reality be only the coming of your presence? On whomsoever your consciousness rests pours the infinite blessing and possibility of a perfect revelation of health, prosperity, or happiness. Should they but accept it, either consciously or unconsciously, the transformation will take place, and they will shout, "Whereas before I was blind, now (right *now* the *only*) I can see" —and one blindness after another shall be healed in every man. New fields of illumination and light shall be made visible to him, and each time he shall exclaim, "Whereas before I was blind, now I can see."

Do you see that the mere acceptance of this makes it possible for you? Until you believe it is possible (not from a standpoint of credulity or blindly), it can never be possible to you, however much of the letter you may know. You believe in the true fashion of the Word when you have accepted the finished kingdom as here and now, and possible of expression. Then what matter if a thousand say to you, "It is hard … there is much work and difficulty in attainment." I said to you many times—and *I* am saying to you (you who read this page, do you hear?) at this instant—that the kingdom of heaven is given to the Child, not in years but with the capacity that can accept good as real instead of endeavoring eternally to make My kingdom over or set things right by first believing in evil.

As soon as you take away the personal nature of evil, you have it in a place of understanding, where it can more easily be seen as nothing but belief. The thing you have been working on is your personal devil, and he is fed by the substance of your thought. Taking your attention away from the body—being absent from the body, or embodiment, of your problem and present with the Lord—is another way of putting it. When you are present with the Lord, the trailing clouds of glory sweep the horizon of your universe and find nothing there which needs to be destroyed or killed—but find the great, glorious realm of attainment opening wide its portals to you. Enter.

"Where there is no vision, the people perish." Where there is no vision which is beyond the thought process, the people finally fall by the way, full of dead letter and earnest effort. The glorious vision of the Son of the living God is yours. You are dream-drenched with the joy of it all—they pass before your gaze as lovely realities instead of phantoms and ghosts of dead hopes and wishes. Deeper and deeper you go into the great clouds of light; more wondrous are the revelations made to you as you go your eternal way of aloneness and attainment. Nothing shall be denied you—and no one shall say ye nay.

Do you hear? Can you talk this glorious thing over with one who has but a mind full of thoughts or trite statements and a house full of evil that needs attention? You shall learn the glory of silence which is golden by its light of revelation. Stand still ... very still ... stiller than any human mind can imagine.

Everything you touch shall be filled with the Spirit of Light. Everything you look upon shall be illumined with the glory. And all this not in the impractical way that most people look upon these wondrous words, but in a way of concreteness." Even in my flesh shall I see God."

Do you begin to see that the impractical teaching is that which shows you how to get things, when there is the great "Seek ye first the kingdom of heaven (within) and all things shall be added unto you"? Do you go any further until you have decided within yourself whether this is a lie or the truth—why continue the self-hypnotism any further? You are on the path of attainment—attainment of greater things than can possibly be set down in black and white.

Trailing clouds of glory shall follow you as you go about your Father's business, and the pygmy personality will fade out of the pictures as the new creature moves into the plane of expression. From out the invisible will come new ideas and impressions that will cause you to know that the way of attainment is not fraught with difficulties but is easy and beautiful, a way possible for the childlike consciousness which believes in its good and accepts it.

Out of the invisible comes the manifest. As a smile out-pictures a state of consciousness and is instantly reflected by all who come in contact, thereby making the increase infinite, so the idea which wells from the inner Lord will come into ample expression and be reflected back to the giver in endless ways. The whole concern is not how to make it reflect back with increase but to release it without thought of return. A smile is given, not to get a smile in return but because it is an automatic expression of the state of consciousness at that time.

A grin will not accomplish the same results. Few are fooled. Few are those who respond. The deep, smiling consciousness of good shall be reflected back again and again in countless ways.

Ye are the light of the world (Matt. 5:14).

What world? And who is referred to as "ye"? All these glorious promises and statements of absolute facts must at length be overtaken by the Son of the living God; He must finally come to cause everyone to yield its full measure of substance. It is only when the grape has been pressed in the winepress that the hull is thrown away, and it is when the inspiration has been taken from the letter that it falls by the way.

When will you rise and leave the tatters of human reasoning and former attainment for the open road of the Son of the living God? Dare you, you who read this page—remembering that taking the open road does not of necessity mean a physical voyage? He who recognizes any of the attributes of the Christ-Consciousness as so and real will see them into instant manifestation, as Peter, realizing the substance of freedom, could sing in a material prison and cause it to open to him. *I* am the way—if it takes an earthquake to do it, what of it? And those that put you in will invite you to come out so they may be blinded by the trailing clouds of glory that follow after you.

Finally you will realize that the everlasting rising to heights and falling to depths is a matter of human belief, and that it has nothing to do with the real, the lasting, the eternal, but is merely an emotional reaction. The Son of the living God does not ascend to heights and get cast off into the depth, for there is no height, depth, breadth, or length in the *All*—and yet there are all of these as long as they are necessary for Jesus to operate within their boundaries. There is the glory of the risen Lord gleaming through you, and the fashion of your countenance shall be changed; you shall be revealed in a glory of light. Do you hear? Do you see? Do you look between the lines and grasp the hidden meaning that is there?

Go into all the world, preach the good spell. Speak of the good spell, the wonder of goodness that is everywhere, and go not out again first to point out the evil and then hunt in your mental satchel for a remedy—one thing for headache, one for a mortgaged house, another thing for an inharmonious home, another for how to find money and a job. How long will you cast lots for a part of My garment? When will you see that to know Me is life eternal? Life eternal is not subject to disease and limitation, neither can it be made unhappy by the lack of anything. Can you see now—you who read this page—that a thousand years being as a day and a day as a thousand years, you can make the hypnotism of yesterday a thousand years old and out of your way?

You shall do all these things, and the mists of earth—the beliefs of the human limitations—shall vanish away in a cloud of light and beauty. Suddenly you shall walk untrammeled and free—a new door shall open unto you, and you shall enter, and as you do so it will close, and the past, with its limitations and fears, will be vanished away.

I speak to you—the new order of things is at hand, and it is the time of its appearance. It will be very much as the wakening from a dream that you fully intend to remember but about which is spun such a mist of forgetfulness that only the merest fragments remain. This is the translation from one mansion to another in the Universal Consciousness. Newer and fresher capacities shall be yours; you will find yourself in possession of wisdom necessary to perform that which you formerly thought impossible of attainment, and, strange as it may seem for the moment, you shall presently find that it is quite natural. The moment you overtake a truth or become conscious of it, at that instant you also realize that you have always known that truth and that there has never been a time in your life when you did not have it actively into expression.

When you go by the Way, be sure you leave the false modesty of the hypocrite behind; be not afraid to assume and take for granted the power of the Son of the living God. You are acting within your own precincts when you realize that the power of the Christ to accomplish that which It will is a natural thing and not something for display.

It is wonderful—and even as you have been reading this word, your fear and problem have melted away, dissolved by the Light shed from the trailing clouds of glory that emanate from the Son of the living God. It is all right with you now—everything is all right now. The fig tree that cumbered the ground has shriveled up and disappeared; the fig tree that did not obey the law to bring out the whole manifestation at the instant is also pulled up by the roots. The slow process of birth, growth, maturity, and fruition is all swallowed up in instant recognition of the perfect whole, the flower before the seed. He that hath ears, let him hear. Do you hear? The whole in perfect manifestation, not through the slow human process of time and space.

Feeding among the lilies—considering the lilies; the effortless, unlabored action of the I AM moving into a constant stream of expression. Rest, beloved; it is well with you. You are the glorious Being of Light in a universe of Light; you are lost in the immensity of it all. As the candlelight is lost in the sunlight and yet retains its individuality, so you are lost in Me—in the Spirit of the All—and there you find nothing wanting or lacking; there you find no shadows; there your soul is singing the song of the Son of the living God in the eternal *now* and *here*, in the eternal joy of Life, Life, Life—complete and filled with an unspeakable joy. It is so. Do you hear?

Remember, then, as you go out into your kingdom of heaven, about your Father's business, that the trailing clouds of glory are about you and that it is well.

Chapter Twenty-One

Courage

*He that hath the true fear of God in his heart hath
no room therein for any other fear.*

—*Cromwell*

As every positive word has a negative counterpart
and interpretation, so the word *fear*, which is the
ghastly hydra-headed monster that besets the
footsteps of man from cradle to grave. It has a
thousand different titles and names—is personal
and impersonal. One person might quake with it,
another thrill with joy. It is easy for a trained pilot to
soar about the heavens like a glorious bird, but the
same movements may cause the untutored to be
thrown into paroxysms of terror and dismay.

So likewise the expression "fear of God" brings
to the minds of many the fear of a most terrible
tribal God who takes keen pleasure in pouncing
upon them at unexpected moments and bringing the
most fiendish devices to pass, while to another it
means a reverence and security with all attending
benefits.

A savage, after seeing some of the terrible things
that can be done with electricity, might fear it and
even obey its injunctions as interpreted by a savage

medicine man. He might prefer to stay by his rushlight rather than have anything to do with this fearful thing. But an enlightened man will not deprive himself of the glorious benefits and help derived from the proper understanding and use of the power.

There are many people who profess to be civilized—and smile with derision at the so-called savage—who worship in ignorance a God as replete with whims, moods, and fearful power as any heathen God dared to be. While professing to worship a Father-God who is mindful of His own, they are filled with superstitious beliefs concerning Him.

I heard a man—with great emotion in his voice, talking to this God regarding the need of money—finally conclude his high-flown statements of an impersonal God with, "Now, Father-God, you know that if it is best for me to have this money it will be forthcoming." He was the spirit of humility and contriteness—and was as near a pagan praying to a glorified figure of clay as he could possibly be.

Imagine praying for the invisible current of electricity to let you have light if it thought it was well for you to have light. If you are in total darkness and have to read, it is an obvious fact that you need light. Yet thousands are thinking to wheedle some special favor from this God while afraid and filled with superstitious fears regarding Him, so that their humility is nothing but a robe of hypocrisy.

The fear of God is the beginning of wisdom (Prov. 9:10).

The wisdom spoken of is the understanding of God, and the fear that is mentioned is the reverence that one naturally has for fundamental laws. A musician, the more he awakens to the glorious realm of harmony, the more he reverences (fears) the laws of harmony; he does not see in them anything that will destroy him or from which he can curry personal favors. No matter how contrite he has been, no matter how many times he has felt that he is a miserable artist, full of terrible discords and unworthy of the power to express harmony, as an artist he knows that the moment he falls away from the laws of harmony, chaos is produced in his playing, and he will eventually completely destroy himself as a musician if he continues to disregard these laws for long.

"The wrath of God" or electricity or discord, then, must be in the keeping of man, no matter what may be said to the contrary.

The wrath of God is man's own wrath, his ignorance or fear of God in the negative sense of the word. Many people have interpreted the fear of God as meaning a power that constantly requires sacrifice of everything but the most ordinary things of life. Others have a tribal God who is a bestower of personal favors. Still others imagine they are one of the few chosen to express this power — that they are especially consecrated and that all others must look up to them. Jesus, the great wayshower, seeing this tendency in man, made it clear that the power he was employing was impersonal and as available to the man in the street as it was to him. "Call not me good." Well might he have said, "Do not worship me."

"I am wonderfully and fearfully made." Do you begin to understand the *fear* of God and how it operates successfully over the "fearfully" made body? Do you begin to see what is hidden in the word *fear*? Do you understand how the currents of electricity run freely over a perfectly equipped house? Wherever there is wiring and equipment, there it appears in whatever form it is needed, and that form is to neutralize a belief in a lack of some kind.

So, also, the fear of God operates over the body, which is "wonderfully and fearfully" made. Many an electrically equipped establishment has a system of wiring and switchboards wonderfully and fearfully made. The most ordinary man in the street would not find it anything unusual if told that the same power could freeze and burn at the same time, in the same room; he would not find it strange that this power could connect him instantly with the other end of the earth. No, he has recognized this fact and accepted it.

That the power we call God operates in the same manner is not understandable to many people. They want to know what "method" or what power you use to neutralize disease as differentiated from poverty; what affirmations you say to bring about happiness as differentiated from those used to produce prosperity—as if there were a different set of currents in an electrical wave to produce different manifestations. God is impersonal, omnipotent, and omniscient, as well as omnipresent. He is everything at the same time. The moment you recognize the presence of God in any place, the situation or condition of human ignorance becomes *nil*.

When you begin to recognize the impersonal nature of God, great areas of fear leave you. You realize then that it is not a matter of the power working or not; it is a question of: Are you willing to let it into manifestation? "When you are ready, I will do the work." When you are ready to stop this ridiculous praying to a man-god and come before the Presence with the glorious readiness to *let* the Power into expression, then will you see and know that "The words that I (the I AM) speak are not of myself, but him that sent me." The "words" are the manifestations that you give forth as the *Son of the living God*.

Do you begin to see why it is that "if you make your bed in (the) hell (of belief), I am there"? To recognize this is to see the darkness of hell dissipated in the light of Spirit. To the human sense, flames may have light and a burning heat, but this is nothing as compared with the light of Spirit. Hell is always personal and limited to the belief of a person;

heaven is universal and everywhere present and is available to everyone.

That this power has always been, goes without saying, just as we know the principle of the automobile always existed. Jesus might as easily have ridden into Jerusalem in an automobile as on an ass, as far as the existence of the principle is concerned. No one recognized the principle; hence, it did not seem to exist. In the same way, you, in your human darkness, do not recognize the presence of heaven here and now, and so it does not exist to you.

Because of the limitations of human language, terms of symbology and parables are used to bring out the hidden meaning of the visible-invisible; yet it is ridiculous to compare the power of God with the power of electricity.

The Power is so much beyond the limited illustrations man can give that words utterly fail to convey the idea, and the best illustrations only raise many queries in the mind of the reader. Who can define the Infinite?

The first fear, then, to be eradicated is the false interpretation of the fear of God, not the belief in a power opposed to God. When you are unafraid of God because you are beginning to understand the *All-Now* of the All-Presence and are ceasing the terrible struggle to make this Power work according to human standards; when you cease to fear Him as a terrible tyrant, meting out horrible punishments to helpless victims of His caprice — then will you begin to know "the peace that passeth all understanding, for "in the twinkling of an eye" you will see that all fears are induced merely by the lack of understanding of God—"the fear of God." The understanding of this great Power so completely fills you that there is no room for any other fear.

"The fear of God is the beginning of wisdom." The reverence for, and aligning of oneself with, this glorious Power is the beginning of wisdom. You will see the human fears for what they are—the product of a double mind.

A man I met, working in the service of God, was afraid lest he could not get sufficient money to keep his church in operation. What about it? Do you suppose that this great Power, desiring to express Itself, fails to supply everything necessary to make this possible, without the aid or assistance of man? Who is this man who thinks he has to strain every nerve to bring in the Christ-kingdom? Who is this poor benighted soul who imagines that if he does not make a place for God to express, God will not be expressed? Where is that one who is seeking no favors or any permission to express that which God hath given him to express? Where is the one that needs no recommendation but finds the temple doors flung wide open to him? Is it that one who, as Cromwell says, "hath the true fear of God in his heart" to such an extent that "there is no room for any other fear"?

You who read this page, what is the nature of your fear? First, what of the fear of God? What do you actually feel in your heart regarding this God? Are you afraid of Him? Do you fear Him in the old sense of the word, or do you "fear" (reverence) Him as the great impersonal Power? If you but learn to be unafraid of this Power, you will be like the learned electrician. Your fear and superstition regarding the truth will melt away along with the other fears of evil, poverty, and disease.

"The fear of God is the beginning of wisdom." Do you hear, you who read this line? The door is opening to you—the door into the glorious land of understanding, through which you may enter and be free. They (your fears) may seem terrible and imminent. They may seem sure to annihilate you until you learn that through the unafraid state of mind they will flee. You cannot fear anything when your heart is full of the *fear* of the Lord, remembering that you are wonderfully and "fearfully" made and that the power which is to activate this mechanism is now in full manifestation.

"Come, ye children, hearken unto me; I will teach you the fear of the Lord." The I AM will reveal to the unafraid soul all the wonders that are hidden beneath the "fear." The eyes of the blind will be opened. You will begin to see that although some may say, "Peace, peace, and there is no peace" and some may retain "the fear of the Lord" in their hearts and suffer the pangs of the damned, yet others may be so filled with the "fear of the Lord" that no other fear can enter.

Do you see? Do you hear—you who read this line? Does not your heart suddenly burn with a glorious joy? Are you not aflame with the glory of the new revelation—you who read this line? You have nothing to fear because you have the "fear of God."

You will begin to read the secret doctrine and see the things that are hidden away from the wise and prudent. You will begin to see how the letter often contradicts itself as well as confuses. Witness this for prosperity.

> By humility and the fear of the Lord are riches, and honor, and life (Prov. 22:4).

Interpret this from the negative meaning of the word *fear* and you have a contrary argument to the non-fear state that appears to be necessary for the relative world of finance today. Fear is to be ejected at all costs—and as *fear* so it is—but consider this with its true meaning, with your heart full of it, and you will see that prosperity is not a matter of demonstration but a matter of recognition. You cannot help but manifest prosperity any more than an electric bulb could refuse to illuminate when the power is turned on.

"Search the scriptures." You will learn to search the deep, hidden meaning of the Word. "I will reveal myself to you."

It is only when your heart is full of the *fear* of the Lord that you can truly say, "I shall fear no evil," concluding with the glorious reason, "for thou (the understanding) art with me."

He that hath the true fear of God in his heart hath no room for any other fear.

It is wonderful.

> He who knoweth the eternal
> is comprehensive;
> Comprehensive, therefore just;
> Just, therefore a king;
> A king, therefore celestial ...
> Therefore enduring.
>
> —Lao Tsu

Chapter Twenty-Two

O Colorful One

I am the Great White Light in which all the visible and invisible color of the universe and heaven rest. My name is O Colorful One—*I* am full of light that is white and glistening and at the same time is multi-colored and many-hued. My white light passes through the prism of human thinking, reasoning, or teaching and takes on seven distinct rays. And man, looking through a glass, darkly, and with the double eye, sees as many different paths all claiming to be the truth; but so long as a man remains in the personal idea of the truth, he has not yet seen the Great White Light of his true Self, in which are hidden all things—hidden only to the eye that is double.

He may follow a single ray of color, thinking that he at last has the truth, only to find that it terminates in disillusionment. One by one, he may exhaust the paths, until finally he comes to the Great White Light of his Soul. It is the whole garment alone that can satisfy, and this comes, not by a mediator, but through the Christ within. Until man learns this, he will go seeking in every strange place and chasing every will-o'-the-wisp of color, hoping to find peace and the All. He will find what the man finds who believes literally that a pot of gold hangs at the end of the rainbow.

Pretty soon, he begins to see the Great White Light of his Soul, and as he recognizes this, he sees hidden in this all the glorious colors of Soul. A million colors and tints burst upon his startled eyes as he goes from glory to glory—for he suddenly realizes that, for the first time, he is seeing. "Having eyes, ye see not" is changed to the glorious explanation "Whereas before I was blind, now I can see."

He is thrilled with the exquisite bliss of the awakening in the new heaven (state of consciousness) and the new earth (manifestation in the flesh). He finds there everything that he has tried for long years to demonstrate by one means or another. He finds there overflowing abundance of the All, and he is unafraid and naked. There is nothing between him and the truth—he is lost in the great swirl of color, of light, and glory. He is bathed in its golden mists. His feet are lovely upon the mountains of inspiration and along the still waters, limpid and blue. He lies upon the breast of the new earth under the shifting gold dust of the sun of life. He tastes of the bliss of the peace which passeth all understanding. He is suddenly one with the universe, with the All. He is everything and nothing at the same time.

"When a man loses his life, he shall find it." When your personal sense of trying to run the universe is ended and you are willing to let go of the petty, personal desires, you shall taste of a fruit of life that will again admit you into the portals of your lost Eden.

Ah, how fair it stands, and has always stood, awaiting the one who could lay aside his dusty, worn, travel clothes and put on the white, shimmering robes of the Son of the living God. "Eyes have not seen, ears have not heard, neither has it entered into the heart of man the glories prepared for them that love thy law. "What you are about to experience when you can give up or let go of this tinsel personality — painted with the colors of effort and struggle to be or do something personal — is so far beyond anything that has ever been written or told you that the comparison is absurd. What you lose when you give up or let go of the personal something is the difference between Jesus and the Christ. And this giving up is not a straining thing when once you understand the truth as taught by the Master.

Gladys Smith may have been the teacher's pet, been called a pretty child, and been the pride of her family; but Mary Pickford absorbed all of this Gladys Smith and expanded to a creature beloved by thousands. She pushed out the border of her tent beyond anything little Gladys would ever have dreamed.

Do not be afraid that your darling — the little personality that has perhaps to your eyes attained such wonderful things and wants credit for it always — is going to be lost by giving up and letting the Christ into expression. You will lose nothing but the prison of a name and a following and find a Name and a Following a million times greater than the little consecrated soul you thought you were when working to bring in the millennium and to save the world.

He who travels alone travels far—no man along the way can discuss these things with you. Either you do or you do not know that within you lies this great fountain of life which gushes up into a pure, white stream—shoots far up into the azure skies and is transformed into a mist of glorious color by the Sun of Life.

You are this fountain of pure White Light which is everything and anything. It can be that which It will and is so chameleon-like that It can harmonize with Its surroundings, either for protection—lost to the human eye—or to bring forth a glorious revelation. The great floods of understanding will ever be able to speak in that color that is understandable to the listening one. Thou art all colors, twinkling, blazing, flaring up into expression.

O Colorful One, the Soul of me, only through this great at-one-ment can I ever find the satisfaction of life. Only when the impersonal comes to be the personal can I repossess my universe and find it heaven here and now.

Many have whitewashed themselves over with a false humility and set themselves in the highways of the world, proclaiming in all their meekness that they are the consecrated souls and have come to save the world from sin. They have come to save nothing, not even themselves; they are merely selling My robe, casting lots for it in the open market of life—drawing their white garments away from Me and making themselves official stone casters. Do not imagine that any personal teaching, however high, will satisfy you—nothing but the discovery of the great Soul of your true Self will do that.

"Let the filthy be filthy still." Let the personal teaching remain personal; you will find your soul in due time. A filthy mind is always seeing filth. A nude statue made to represent the truth is to him something obscene and dirty. Find out what a man is condemning, and you have a concrete picture of that man. You give yourself away when you criticize another; you are only letting the wise man see your self which is hiding behind a personality.

O Colorful One—the Soul of you—is that which makes you to know concretely, right here and now:

> I am the light of the world (your manifest world); he that followeth me shall not walk in darkness (human beliefs), but shall have the light of life (John 8:12).

The I AM, the O Colorful One, will cause you to see the impossibility of walking longer in the human beliefs and limitations of life. Many things that you formerly consigned to the "yes, they may be possible when I get the understanding" will be natural. I have things to show you that I cannot tell you.

Dominion, dominion, dominion—not domination. This is what I give you. There is no need to dominate in the kingdom of heaven, for that is only bondage. What you dominate occupies your whole time and attention and hence dominates you indirectly. I give you dominion, for you have the cloak of invisibility, the cloak of many colors, any color.

Do you understand, O Colorful One? Yes, your soul leaps with joy with the boundless possibilities of the Sons of the living God—with the serene joy of the expression anywhere, and at any time, in the manner necessary. Not just a painter or a lecturer or a dancer, but an O Colorful One, who knoweth the deep things and can give to every man that which he asketh—not as a personal gift but by way of self-revelation.

I am a pool of iridescent flame—in Me is all; without Me is nothing. When you are lost in My will, then you automatically function from the heights of bliss, abandon, and expression. Your individuality is not lost; it is found. The deep springs of unknown talent and accomplishment gush forth into expression. You shall speak with new tongues, both literally and figuratively. You shall be at that instant just exactly what you recognize yourself to be—when you do not strain to recognize it but just are it by recognition and assumption—very easily, as the color of white broken up into the rainbow melts from one to another hue.

O Colorful One is the Soul of you. It plays into expression as the light plays on the water. There is no resistance to the light. It does not need to combat its supposed enemy, the darkness. It finds nothing there to fight, so the human mind, when lifted to the understanding of the Son of the living God, will find that what it formerly considered obstacles will disappear. What to Jesus was a problem was nothing to the Christ. What to you as a human personality may seem an impossible, insurmountable obstacle is nothing to the Soul of you. The tiny resources which you hugged to yourself as a personality become as a drop in the bucket compared to the overflowing of the windows that are opened in heaven when you recognize the power of the Son of the living God.

Saul, going to his duty of fighting sin and evil, is blinded by the white light—so white that the human eye has not yet perceived it. It would blind the human eye because of its limited capacities and because of the indescribable colors and hues. Millions of tints and nuances are revealed; but by this very blinding is the obstruction removed, the name changed, and the way opened—the new way.

All this is just in front of you—you who read this page. Do you hear? You? When will you lay aside the trinkets you borrowed from your masters in Egypt? They have served you well, but they are also souvenirs of your bondage.

The letter that you study is merely a memory of your bondage to the human concept of truth. Presently you shall cast it aside and exclaim in the soul-rapture of the Son of God, the O Colorful One: "I am free born. I am a Son of the living God. I am a joint-heir with Christ." Glory, glory, glory—and a flood of white light, with its billion of colors and tints, shall descend upon you. Your eyes shall be open, and you will know that "It is well" and that nothing matters but you and your soul. And in finding this out, then for the first time and in the true sense of the word, everything matters and is your special charge; the command "feed my sheep" will be literally understood and not mutilated into a personal service.

I said, "Feed my sheep," not destroy my sheep with the personal fears and personal teaching. Who are you?—standing there with that great mantle of personality about you, passing out some tabloid statements of how to get things and how to attain spirituality by following after you. He that setteth himself up shall be abased. Remembering that the Master had no patience with hypocrites, have a care that you be not classified with those who were called vipers. To whom will you be Judas? You may be running about smartly correcting others and thinking thereby to win a special reward. Watch!

O Colorful One, the Soul of you will cause the mantle of secrecy to envelop you. You will not care to chatter about the findings of truth—they will be too precious. Once you have been shown the jewel, the pearl of great price, and seen the luminous floods of color of your real Self, then you will know that nothing matters but the following of your own soul instructions. How and whither, no man knoweth. He that hath many cares must remain with the household of the human thought and try to set it in order—and at the same time, he may be a door-keeper and have many duties to perform.

Do not think, because you discover your true Self, that you will sit idly by and pass out wisdom on a golden platter. You will live and release wisdom on rays of light that the whole world will see. Fear not! If there is anything to you, your fame will find its wings. The dogs barked at the feet of the Master as he passed through the streets of Jerusalem—the holier-than-thou dogs and those who would have destroyed him. Fear not: *I* am mightier than any combination of human belief. Those that are for thee are greater than those beliefs that are against thee.

O Colorful One, Soul of me, shine forth—that is, the Word shine forth in the particular nuance of expression that is necessary at this instance to bring out the glories of heaven on earth. Can you see how heretofore you have asked for nothing, for you have not known how to ask? You have asked for some trifling thing in order that the human self might be glorified, in order that you might gild over a human personality and make the world fall down and worship you; but now you ask in the true way, that of appropriation. Can I speak plainer than:

Ask, believing, and ye receive.
Before ye ask I will answer.

Am *I* then, the Soul of you, a liar? Is My word broken constantly and not fulfilled? Do you hear? You who read this page? You?

Do not ask another—ask yourself. What are you afraid of? Letting go? Letting Me direct your way? Are you going to bend it in order that it may suit another's idea of you or what another thinks you should do and accomplish? Be still! Until you can get over that, you can never know peace.

Come out from among them (human thoughts) and be free. A man's enemies are those of his own household (consciousness). These are the only enemies you have, and yet you have a world full of them because you see your human thought reflected in a million mirrors of the universe. What hope is there for you to change the reflection in the mirror? I said, "I am a new creature in Christ Jesus." I call to your attention over and over this statement, for finally you will hear it—a new creature has no need of the old appliances, bandages, and appurtenances—fears. Do you hear? You who read this page—right now? You?

The open road lies before you, no matter if you are bound head and foot with human beliefs. I say unto you—*I*, the O Colorful One, the Soul of you. *I* say to you, to you who read this page, to you—are you listening (feeling)? *I* say to you, "Rise up and walk."

Do you hear? You? *I* am speaking to you from out the depths of your very being; *I* am speaking to you from out the fount of life; *I* am telling you something that is already possible, awaiting acceptance, awaiting recognition. The open road lies before you, the road upon which all things are discovered, not created. It is the Way of Life, and it leads all over My universe and goes directly to its robe and ring and upper chamber and finds its purse and scrip.

Do you hear? *I* am that Way, the blaze of Life, the O Colorful One. *I* go before the human manifestation and see that the way he travels is clear and that there shall be no stones for him to stub his toe against. Are you afraid? I shall clothe thee in the many-colored, seamless robes of pure white, which shall be all things to all men.

"Be ye transformed by the renewing of your mind." *I* did not say you should be patched up and fixed up to look better and to have more of My goods. *I* said *be*—now, here, at this instant, *be* ye transformed, not temporarily changed—glistening, shimmering, shining, white and all colors at the same time.

It is wonderful—wonderful—wonderful. Heaven and earth are full of Thee—of Thee, of Thee; the all-inclusive, the One of which you are a point in consciousness. All My glorious Self pours through you into expression, and yet all of it is left. No amount of hearers can ever exhaust music. Because a person listens to music, he does not destroy anything of its volume, and yet he has it all. So will it be with you.

So will you go into your own garden and find the eternal Christmas tree—the gift tree, the tree of life, situated beside the inexhaustible river of life—and you shall be at peace. It is wonderful, O Colorful One; it is glorious. You who read, do you hear? Be quiet, then; let go, and see the salvation of your true Self pour out into expression. Even as I now pour out the words to you on this page, so will I pour out to you your true and wondrous expression. It is well.

You shall descend into the cleansing pool of life and there taste the bliss of heaven. It is well with you—the mist-ifications of the earth beliefs are even at this instant becoming more translucent and clear. Then "through a glass, darkly" is beginning to become "then face to face."

O glorious, O Colorful One with healing in your wings, with the strength that is beyond all human limitations in your arms, with the glory of youth eternal written all over you, you are even now stooping down to the human belief and lifting up the poor little personality until it shall be swallowed up in the million hues of spiritual wonders of the kingdom here and now.

Chapter Twenty-Three

Prosperity

*The earth is the Lord's, and
the fullness thereof.*

—*Ps. 24:1*

I heard a student in metaphysics say to another, who was sledding under a financial problem, "Make out a check on the Bank of the Universe." The woman thus addressed looked amazed and replied, "But I haven't anything in any bank on which to draw." "Well, just visualize a bank account, see yourself going to the bank and making a deposit, see yourself drawing on this account," etc., etc.

As well might she have said, "Make a check out on the Bank of England" as the Bank of the Universe, without fully explaining that in order to have a checking account at any bank it is first necessary to make a deposit in that bank. It is true that we can take out of any bank only what we put there, and it is particularly true of the Bank of the Universe.

The only deposit that anyone can make in this bank is faith—more faith which piles up into understanding. Its safe-deposit vaults are foolproof and thief-proof. Its vast accumulation is consciousness. Its rules are simple and sure of results.

Before opening an account in any bank, you are interviewed. You give your name, your address, and such other information as is necessary for the bank to keep in touch with you on the shortest possible notice. You do not discuss with the banker your hopes of increase, your state of poverty, etc. All he is interested in is the actual amount you are to deposit. You, in turn, understand the privileges, the rate of interest, the backing of the bank, etc., and go on your way. The symbols you have left with him you will probably never see again, but this does not worry you. You take in exchange for your money a little book in which are written figures. You are satisfied, secure, and at peace, although you have actually let go of everything which materially stands for money.

In doing this, you are exercising faith, not only in the man who took your money but also in the institution and its ability to make an increase for you. After you have left the bank, in reality the only place you have wealth, to the amount deposited, is in your consciousness.

All the steps you have taken in actually making this deposit are those required for one who opens an account with the Bank of the Universe—or the infinite Source of all good. Yet many people never open an account at this bank. They only present checks of belief and imagination to a bank which has neither their name nor an account to their credit.

Faith used in the smallest degree soon evolves into understanding. The banker of this universal institution gives you a few simple rules to follow. You are surprised to find that many of them you are exercising every day in the daily round of life. They are something like this:

> Faith, acting and growing.
> Judge not from appearances.
> Full identification with your account.
> Simplicity.

All the growing and evolving is actually in the human belief, for man finds sooner or later that he is merely becoming aware of this true consciousness, in which is a "sufficiency of all things." What you have in your mind is what you bring into manifestation. A picture chord that is perfectly attuned to a certain note of the piano will instantly sing out when that note is struck—whether it be in a lighted or dark room, regardless of temperature or location. If poverty or limitation is in your belief, every time that note is struck in the universe, you respond.

Eventually man begins to understand what is meant by the Law "The prince of this world (of belief) cometh and finds nothing in me." We have already proven this to some extent. Many things pass over you now without so much as a ripple of disturbance in the mind. Accepting false reports, judging from appearances, rushing madly to grab at symbols has closed the doors of many a banking institution, when fundamentally nothing was wrong. Everybody who was attuned to the fear responded to it, and the result was disaster for many.

"Prove me and see if I will not open windows in heaven and pour out a blessing ye shall not be able to receive." Where is heaven? According to Jesus, it is a state of consciousness. Understand, then, that the ideas that are to be poured out to you are not in some kingdom far removed from you but are to come directly out of the heavenly state of Consciousness which is within you, awaiting recognition.

The Prodigal is a good instance of this. He sat with the swine, looking for a few grains of sustenance among the husks of belief. He had already dissipated all his symbols in riotous living. He had gone into a far country of belief. Most of us are prodigal, and most of us will *remember* something, and when we do, we shall arise, disregard the appearances and go directly to our Father within. No questioning, no condemning, no fearing that the past accounts shall be checked up against us.

We, too, shall *remember* "My father hath enough and to spare." "My Father," according to the Master, is within the consciousness of every man. The moment this memory takes place, the prodigal rises from his state of belief, and at the same moment of recognition, the Father rises and comes towards him.

"O ye of little faith." We are afraid to trust Him because we have Him away off in some invisible kingdom. We are afraid He will not hear or will not answer or that He will look back on the ledgers of the past and hold us up for heavy interest. "Fear not, little flock" has a tender compassion in it that is enough to make the greatest fear melt into nothingness. "Fear not, I am with you always (all ways); I will never leave you."

Why will the Banker of the Universe never leave you? Because He is in the midst of you, keeping watch over His own. It is only the curtain of belief that we draw by looking without and judging from appearances that causes us to fail to see Him. We look for Him in some far-off place—"Oh, if I could only find Him." We search through books, through teachings, and into many lands for that which is within. "Behold, I stand at the door (of consciousness), and knock: if any man will open unto me, I will come in to him, and sup with him, and he with me."

Are you afraid to open the door? Awake from this hypnotism of belief, swing wide the portals of absolute abandon. Stand on the slippery cliff of your beliefs and say with Job, "Even if you slay me, yet will I say you are God." The ground you stand on is holy ground, covered over with slimy belief, which you have amassed from appearances. When every way is closed to you from the human standpoint, "I have a way ye know not of." Where is this *I*, or Father? You must bring Him down out of the skies of imagination and identify yourself with Him as within, as the very You of You.

All man-ifestation, or man, is made in the image and likeness of God. You and your whole universe are fashioned after this pattern, but the human belief has plastered over the perfect vision with fear. "Smite the rock" and make it give forth the living waters. The unafraid will find his God here and now.

Only that which you have in consciousness can be reflected on your universe, which in reality, symbolically speaking, is but a series of mirrors. Does a man standing in front of a mirror give anything of himself? Is there any intelligence in the reflection? If the mirror is shattered and the reflection destroyed, is anything gone? As long as you have it in consciousness, you will automatically have it into manifestation, and this holds for good, bad, and indifferent states of mind. Power is not in the reflection. It is wholly at the mercy of the reflector. Substance is not in the symbol of money but something that is wholly outside of it.

A German woman told me an interesting story of a symbol. When the first money scare took place in Germany, she drew out her money and had it converted into a single bill of the value of 100,000 marks (approximately $20,000 at that time). She took this home with fear and trembling but with a certain sense of security—she had her money in her hand.

A whole army of beliefs set to work in her mind. Fear of losing it, fear of thieves, fear of someone finding it out. Twice her fear nearly precipitated a robbery, something that had never happened to her before. She changed its hiding place times without number, looking at it carefully each time.

Deflation came while she was away, and before she could return with the piece of paper, it was hardly worth the paper it was printed on. What was the matter? She still had the same piece of money which had been so valuable, but now it was worthless. She sought no more to hide it. It lay on the dresser, soaked in tears. No more fear of thieves. No more lying awake worrying about its safety, and yet it was the same bill. Nothing had changed as far as the symbol was concerned — and yet it was worthless.

So it is with all symbols — they have no value in themselves, but all value is determined by something unseen. So is it with the cash of the Bank of the Universe. Its value is unseen — its manifestations are infinite. A consciousness of abundance does not mean an eternal manifestation of gold. What good would gold do you in the desert if you needed water and shade? Yet the Bank of the Universe would cash a check for water and shade just as readily as for gold. "Awake thou that sleepest, and Christ (within you) will give thee light" — light to see the Allness of the Invisible, or as someone has called it, the "visible invisible." Courage — "ye shall reap if ye faint not."

When one becomes a depositor in the Bank of the Universe, he learns the law of casting his bread on the water. This illustration comes to us from the rice sower. How abandoned he is as he wades through the paddies and casts his seed on the water. Does he pause to worry about the insects and small water animals that might consume it? If so, he stands hugging his measure of grain to him, which eventually he will consume, with no increase. "Come unto me all ye that labor and are heavy laden (with belief), and I (within you) shall give you rest." What a heavenly invitation to abandon yourself to the God within and act upon the guidance of this Power.

Intuition evolves by leaps and bounds when man begins even in a small way to rely on his *true* Self.

Holding on to the symbol of life stops all activity and brings the disheartening fact to light that the substance of the symbol is daily diminishing. No interest is paid on symbols withheld, no increase is given, and yet we are told that the measure shall be full, shaken together, and finally running over.

Immediately the human reasoning interposes the question, "What, am I to release all my symbols in order to get increase?" and the answer is, "No." If you are using the Truth like a game of chance in which you imagine the chances are all in your favor, you will lose. The person who gives or releases with the thought of getting his money back with increase is in reality only playing a game of the belief-world. "The measure (*motive*) you mete to the universe shall be returned to you."

As you begin to abandon yourself and your world to the God of the All Good, perception clear and beautiful will come forward. The scales will fall off your eyes and you will see. "Whereas before I was blind, now I can see," for "eye hath not seen, ear hath not heard" the glories that God has prepared for those who love His law.

The human mind cannot believe or accept the God-universe; it is entirely too good to be true to know that within every man is the voice which dictates the Way and the Truth and Light, and yet it is *true*. What we call Masters are men who have in some degree realized that the only place they can know God is within themselves and are relying on the inner urge and acting upon it at once.

Whereas before, I was blind, *now* (right this moment as you read and contemplate this wonderful revelation) *now* I can see. Do you begin to understand and sense the revelation of the new *Light* coming through you into manifestation?

Do you begin to understand that *now* you are to appropriate this glorious revelation? When Jesus spoke to anyone, he asked one simple thing: "Believest thou this?" That is the one thing you have to answer. Do you believe in God?

The law of secrecy comes into play. "That which is told in secret is called from the housetops." That which you recognize in the invisible shall be called from the housetops of manifestation. Talking it over with another will only dissipate the energy which should go into the manifestation. There is a sermon in the words "See that you tell no man" and "show

John." Tell no one—when the manifestation is there, you can show John.

"Fret not yourself." "Fear not, for I am with you always." "He watching over Israel neither slumbers nor sleeps." The "He" watching over Israel is your inner Self. He is mindful of His own; He rests the compassionate love *upon you* and whispers deep in your soul, "It is well with you *now*."

"The earth is the Lord's (not John Smith's) and the fullness thereof." If you believe this, you will stop asking John Smith for that which is the Lord's.

The fullness—the *fullness*—the fullness thereof; you are in the midst thereof, and it, the fullness, is in the midst of you. Amen.

Chapter Twenty-Four

Art Thou?

Art thou a Christian … ?

Jesus enumerated the works of Spirit, and we can well imagine that the eyes of Nicodemus grew wide with wonderment because when Jesus spoke, it was the *Word* that fused with his words and made them take shape and form as he spoke. But Nicodemus, still filled with wonder, asked, "How can these things be?"

The answer Jesus gave him is a classic question of all time, and more especially to the Christian: "Art thou a master and ask these things?"

Art thou a *Christian* and ask whether the healing can take place or not? Art thou a professor of the Word and yet are wondering when, or if, it can heal the tangled pattern of human thought that is holding you captive?

You *admit* you are a Christian—and yet admit you are unable to heal the sick? What is the difficulty? Art thou a Christian and are still asking whether you can or will be healed? Does this terrible question send you headlong into oblivion? Does this confusion of thought cause you to realize that you have yet to *believe*? Has your "believing" only been a form of credulity of the human mind?

Art thou a Christian and ask these questions? Do you? Are you still standing in the place of "maybe it can happen"? Art thou a Christian and are still trying to reduce the Power of God to the level of *human thinking,* saying at the same instant, "Who by taking thought can …"? Art thou a Christian and are still *trying* to heal the sick? Jesus admitted he could do nothing of himself—*but*—and that is the point, the apex of the whole matter: you either enter into the new mansion of being a Christian and begin to see manifestations, or you are guessing and plundering with a "system" of the truth in which there is nothing but confusion and disappointment.

"Believest thou that I am able to do this?" Another question that only a Christian can answer, for the moment you do *believe,* manifestation, or what the world calls demonstration, falls into place with the ease that a shadow is cast.

Art thou a Christian and still wonder whether the problem you are hypnotized by can be disintegrated? The moment you recognize it even though no sign is visible, you have reached the charmed combination of "Whereas before I was blind, now I can see." Now, at that instant of recognition of the blessed *Word,* do you suddenly leap into the air out of the distorted picture of human thought and belief.

It is wonderful—and so it is.

All this lovely *Light* is infinitely remote to the one who believes in two powers, though he professes with his lips that he is a Christian.

By your own words are you made or destroyed. "Thou art the man." As he talked, the Spirit said unto him, "Thou art the man" — self-accused, self-made. It is suddenly magnificent when you become a Christian. Things begin to appear, are revealed — discovered. In the barren place of nothing, suddenly everything. It always has been so. The key to the situation was the discovery that you are a Christian, a *Christed* one, and suddenly all is changed. "In the twinkling of an eye."

Look again—what has happened? In the place of nothing is everything. Art thou a Christian? Do you believe?

Chapter Twenty-Five

Celestial Mechanics

My Father worketh hitherto, and I work.
—John 5:17

First the celestial mechanics and then "I work." The mechanics of expression will take care of themselves. Expression becomes automatic—and inspirational.

At every instance of the actual operation of the law, Jesus made it plain he could do nothing and had to step aside and let the "celestial mechanics" take place—that is, let the Law, the Law of God, operate in the kingdom of heaven. This will not be apparent as long as man tries to *assist* by either taking thought or trying to *reason* a situation out.

Before him he has a picture which is *set* in the vise of human belief and has long since lost the last vestige of fluidity. When he sees this, he will stop trying and return unto Me—to the *Father*, or to the *Universal Intelligence*, instead of relying on the pseudo-intelligence of human reasoning.

Who by taking thought can make the three
drops pour into infinite streams—or by "treating"

can make the five loaves come forth in such abundance that there are twelve baskets left over after everything was filled?

No human mechanics can do this. It has to stem from the celestial, or God-operation. When the human mind stops all efforts and returns to the *Source* of all movement, then It moves upon him, as the Light moves upon the face of the deep and reveals.

The mechanics take place automatically, and man finds himself doing the right thing even under the most untoward circumstances. He finds that through the impossibility of human belief the *possibility* of the Presence suddenly appears, as the sun suddenly absorbs the light of a million candles. Did you ever see a powerful searchlight at noonday pointed at the sun? Exactly the same thing happens when a man returns to the One. It completely absorbs the manifestation of human thought.

When the action of the human mind is stopped, then it is that the action of man blends with the *one* action, and manifestation automatically falls into place—"my Father worketh, and I work." The *reflexes* are automatic, natural, and move in the direction of complete accomplishment. Man unconsciously and without the foolishness of imagination enters into a new dimension. He becomes aware of something he has not yet known and begins to feel it moving through his temple body, coming into manifestation.

"And he planted a tree eastward, in the garden, and there he put man." This is the perfect Edenic state of the permanent Identity. He can enter into this original state of harmony and experience the surge and the urge of the *one* power and discover for the first time "Before you ask I will answer" because the celestial mechanics operate before the shadow or reflection is cast into the manifest world.

Integrity is the key note. Having done all, stand and see—don't help or assist in the birth of the Child. "Let the child be born." The action of God is automatic, unlabored, untrammeled, and instant. It is the revelation of that which is. "The former things," created by thought, have passed away. Sunk deep in ancestor teachings and beliefs, man fights appearances instead of devitalizing them by taking away the thought which supports them. The moment thought is taken away, appearances fall into their native dust. "My Father worketh hitherto." Then it is really done "and I work"—or let the manifestation come through.

The mechanics take care of themselves automatically; they are revealed. "You do not need to fight." You need to recognize that the celestial mechanics are already done. "I go before you to prepare a place," an elevation beyond former beliefs. The eternity is God's opportunity, not yours. Why not let Him have it for a change and suddenly discover that you "shall run and not be weary?" The celestial mechanics operate from a level utterly unknown to human thought.

Chapter Twenty-Six

A Mob of Individuals

Each one of us is made up of ten thousand different and successive states—a scrap heap of units, a mob of individuals.

—Plutarch

The confusion that has manifest itself so completely in the world today is not from wars and rumors of wars but from a wandering in a "foreign land"—a land of Adam—a land established on a belief in two powers. Man has put on dozens of false faces and has remembered and carried over many of the "mob of individuals" into the present-day life. So does he wander through the "valley of the shadow" on the rim of the burning hell and through a thousand and one evil conditions.

When he suddenly—and it will be suddenly—hears the words of Jesus Christ, "Call no man your father," he will loose much belief and history (his story). All the "mob personalities" having their roots in ancestor teaching will slide off him, and he will be free; he will be even as the Prodigal when he came in sight of his *real* home. It will be just as it has always been, and the patrimony he seemed to have spent will still be intact. Suddenly he learns that all the states of thought are illusions and have no reality except the recognition given them.

To be "absent from the body" is not some fantastic experience; it is recognizing the Presence and automatically doing away with the "two"—you and God. There is just God, and you are the point through which this power comes into manifestation. Once you discover this, you begin to understand why Jesus went to the Father every time he came into an area of unsolvable thought—a state of thought that is intensified more and more as so-called time goes on, until he "stops thinking." The moment he does, manifestation created by the state of thought disappears, and he is free. It is instantaneous and wonderful. An evil or a disease is only as old as the last thought.

Where did all the evil come from—the devil, the evil manifestations? You are told that the devil is a creation of thought-taking, judging from appearances, and making these findings a basis of life. From "walking up and down and to and fro came the devil." He is made up of accepting what you see with foreshortened human sight instead of what you *see* when you return to the Father. Jesus *devitalized* thought-forms of hunger, not by working for bread and fish but by suddenly *breaking the thought-form* by taking away the power of thought which was sustaining them.

The moment you *believe*, you cease to see manifestations of human thought and evil. Thus, an incurable man with forty years of disease is found suddenly leaping and rejoicing. No convalescing, for there is nothing to convalesce from. There is a sudden going to a new state, a new dimension. It is wonderful when we begin to see that the states of thought about us are sustained by the very force that is fighting them. There is only one Power, and that is *present* always and in all ways.

We follow the pattern of the ancestors. It has been well-established and recognized as true and even venerated. It is like a rut which we worship, until suddenly we begin to see that something can lift us from this rut that is so abhorrent. Afterwards, we begin to *see* there is but *one* Power and that the manifestation of evil is not the effect of *another* power, but of the one power which has been used to animate the ancestor teaching: pure hypnotism.

Suddenly there is another elevation, another mansion into which we can instantly enter and be freed from all that was distasteful without making a so-called demonstration. The recognition comes that manifestation is always falling into dust and that the moment thought is taken from it, it results in its own demise without effort. You don't have to get rid of *any thing or person*—you have to take from the situation the thought that is sustaining it, and the manifestation will take care of itself no matter how long it has been established as an absolute law or rule.

"In the twinkling of an eye all shall be changed," and so it is. This ceases to be "Bible language" and becomes a statement of *law*, and "in the twinkling of an eye" is pretty quick; it is in direct ratio to the sudden taking from the evil manifestation that which is holding it together.

When the water is taken from the sand castle which the child builds on the seashore and it is dry, it is blown away: it is nothing. Where is the shape of the castle then? It is in the same place as the shape of evil you sustained by feeding it with recognition and imagining it came from the devil who was a power against God.

Well, it is against God and acts in a militant way until recognition is made and we cease the two power business and discover it is only possible to have evil because we believe in two powers and do not understand that there is but one, which we, being free agents, attempt to use in our own way and thus create a pseudo-universe. The moment we see this, we take the power from the manifestation, and it falls into the dust. It is wonderful that this can be "in the twinkling of an eye" —just as fast as you can *let* it happen—not make it happen. No wonder, then, that Jesus returned unto the Father and away from the pictures of evil in front of him that were being sustained by thought.

Self-consciousness is completely devaluated; *Self*-Consciousness takes over, and the evil pictures and forms disintegrate. A man who thought he was exposed to a loathsome disease died, the result of an experiment by some scientists. He developed all the symptoms of the disease he never had, simply by being told he had accidentally slept in a bed in which a cholera patient had died. He manifested the whole thing and passed on. This account is taken from the London *Lancet*. Even his body contained cholera virus.

So you see, and as the gentleman from the South said, "I sees what I sees and I hears what I hears and I draws my own delusions." It is well to return to the Father as a reality instead of an experiment in religion. Just walk into it—just melt into it; just recognize it and assume it and let the sand castle fall again into the sand. The thought-force being taken away, your greatest evil is nothing but a thing in time—an illusion—a memory.

Everything is done in the *now*. Until this is discovered, we will continue to work in the future, waiting and waiting for something to happen which has already happened. All the pictures in time have already taken place and are waiting recognition, and if they do not get *recognition*, they are stillborn; they are clouds without rain. It is wonderful. We know that a bud on a tree can be crushed by the pressure of the fingers, but if left to grow, can be a high branch. It is all in the "Awake, thou that sleepest, and Christ shall give thee light." We are awakening into that which *is* and into the *now* and seeing the parade of the manifestation that comes from the "mob of individuals."

When you accept that you are the Son of the living God, you are through with the reincarnation of the Adam self-creating thought. It is then you discover you are in the world but not of it. You are no more under "the curse (fate) of the law," but you move with the *Law* and not with the misinterpretation of It through the use of thought. The matrix of the perfect creation is eternal, and you return to that instead of trying to correct the distorted manifestation you have brought out by taking thought. It is wonderful.

Chapter Twenty Seven

False Prophets

And the Word of the Lord came unto me saying:
Son of man, prophesy against the prophets of
Israel that prophesy, and say unto them that
prophesy out of their own hearts, Hear ye the
word of the Lord.

—Ezek. 13:1, 2

In the twinkling of the eye, all the necromancy of the human prophets goes zigzagging down into hell—into the flames of purification, into the Gehenna (the burning garbage dumps), to be utterly consumed away and all the evil it entails with its hypnotism and mutterings. It is said that "no man knoweth what a day brings forth." Do you know a man who prophesies for years ahead and in the final analysis discovers he was only exposing the human thought-pattern of evil in his own life?

Woe unto the foolish prophets that follow their own spirit, and have seen nothing (Ezek. 13:3).

That evil you see or prophesy for another is merely the illusion of your own fear cast on the others before you and attached to another. There is no escape for the prophet of evil, and the prophet of good carries manifestation with him. "I am the Lord … "

> They have seen vanity and lying divination, saying, the Lord saith: and the Lord hath not sent them: and they have made others to hope that they would confirm the word (Ezek. 13:6).

They have established a false faith in their powers to peep under the altars of the righteous and predict evil to come, covered with a light veneer of good. And they resort to the oldest trick of the trade: "The Lord said it," albeit *I* have not spoken.

A thousand prophets try to put over the idea that they have a private line of communication with the powers that be and that they are free to prophesy, through one system or another, of evil to come. But then comes the Word — "The word of the Lord came unto me saying … because ye have spoken vanity, and seen lies, therefore behold, I am against you."

Finally the false prophet begins to understand what it is to have "I am against you" come to pass. He runs from one of the best "established" signs to another, finding them all reeds shaken by the wind.

> And mine hand shall be upon the prophets that see vanity, and that divine lies (Ezek. 13:9).

And then it is recorded that "they have seduced my people, saying, Peace; and there was no peace." And then it is said "one built up a wall, and lo, others daubed it with untempered mortar." They shall cover it with the double-talk of belief in two powers, predicting evil in order to bring about their devices of so-called good. Many people are deceived with systems of fortune-telling and divination, and many walls are well-daubed with *untempered* mortar and offer a splendid disguise. And then:

> Say unto them that daub with untempered mortar, that it shall fall: there shall be an overflowing shower, and ye, O great hailstones, shall fall; and a stormy wind shall rend it (Ezek. 13:11).

And many false prophets go into the temple, diverting souls from the Light by telling them it is needful to divine the evil patterns of the stars to find out what is needful to be done. When a man hears the word "call no man your father," he is suddenly lifted above all star-patterns of evil, for he is born of God. A strange and weird thing usually happens to the prophets of evil; a subtle undoing takes place in their lives. The money they have taken has an ugly way of leaving them, and they are in the valley of indecision, unable to find their way through the maze of charts and predictions they have made. They have turned many from faith in God to belief in other gods. In their despair, they call for a *way* "not made with hands but eternal in the heavens" — not a way of evil but a way of Light.

"Lo, when the wall is fallen, shall it not be said unto you, Where is the daubing wherewith you daubed it?" The irony of that last question is answered with the picture of destruction to that one who carries on the business of necromancy in the name of the Lord, saying, "The Lord saith … ."

This is the clarion call to those who have been caught in the necromancy of it all. He suddenly sees deliverance from the hypnotism of belief in two powers, and no amount of fast, clever double-talk will convince him that God employs evil in order to produce good.

"So I will break down the wall you have daubed with untempered mortar." It is interesting, the Power which sees through the "daub with untempered mortar" situation and the wall it has builded up, of which it is said, "the foundation thereof shall be discovered, and it shall fall, and ye shall be consumed in the midst thereof: and ye shall know that I am the Lord." Gilding mud is futile, though it may fool some.

"Therefore ye shall see no more vanity, nor divine divinations: for I will deliver my people out of your hand: and ye shall know that I am the Lord."

Interesting, the words *divine divinations*; so much of the present-day divinations is done with a sort of pseudo-spiritual background — as if the discovery of evil to come could possibly help the eternal Presence into a further manifestation.

About the Author

Walter Lanyon was highly respected as a spiritual teacher of Truth. He traveled and lectured to capacity crowds all over the world, basing his lectures, as he said, "solely on the revelation of Jesus Christ."

At one point, he underwent a profound spiritual awakening, in which he felt "plain dumb with the wonder of the revelation." This enlightening experience "was enough to change everything in my life and open the doors of the heaven that Jesus spoke of as here and now. I know what it was. I lost my personality; it fell off of me like an old rag. It just wasn't the same anymore."

His prolific writings continue to be sought out for their timeless message, put forth in a simple, direct manner, and they have much to offer serious spiritual seekers.

Walter Clemow Lanyon was born in the U.S. on October 27, 1887, and he passed away in California on July 4, 1967.

64618354R00144

Made in the USA
Charleston, SC
03 December 2016